Blowing America's Mind

A True Story of Princeton, CIA Mind Control, LSD and Zen

John Selby and Paul Jeffrey Davids

Blowing America's Mind

A True Story of Princeton, CIA Mind Control, LSD and Zen

ISBN #978-0-9970559-9-3

Cover Design by Ron James
On the bench of the cover, Paul Jeffrey Davids (left) and John Selby (right), photo from early 1970's
Back cover lower left: Photo of Nassau Hall, Princeton University

Yellow Hat Publishing
A Division of Yellow Hat Productions, Inc.
5605 Riggins Court #200
Reno, Nevada 89502

The names of characters in this book who are public figures or who have been divulged in news articles about the mind control projects known as MK-ULTRA have not been changed. Some of the Princeton students (apart from the authors themselves) and Anne and Linda are composite characters inspired by people the authors knew. This book adheres as closely as possible to the events actually lived by the authors.

This book is dedicated to all those fallen heroes (and those not-so-heroic) of that first wild rush up 'Psychedelic Hill' – and to the original psychedelic pioneers: Humphry Osmond, M.D., Bernard S. Aaronson, Ph.D. (both of the New Jersey Neuro-Psychiatric Institute and co-authors of the book *Psychedelics*); to Aldous Huxley (who opened his mind using mescaline with the help of his guide Dr. Osmond and wrote *The Doors of Perception*); professor Timothy Leary, Ph.D., who was fired from Harvard for his psilocybin experiments using undergraduates (and who permitted Paul Davids in 1996 to make an authorized biographical documentary, *Timothy Leary's Dead)*; Alan Watts, who supported and guided John Selby through hard times; and of course Albert Hofmann, who invented LSD and was the first to experience its power in 1943. May they all rest in peace and be remembered.

Acknowledgments

The authors acknowledge all the publishers who turned down early drafts of this book, beginning with its first incarnation in 1973. When Mel Gibson starred in "Conspiracy Theory" (a motion picture intended as the ultimate statement about CIA mind control and MK-ULTRA) the authors put their still-unfinished manuscript aside and waited another twenty years before bringing this historic memoir into public view.

The authors also acknowledge the patience of their friends and families in awaiting the eventual publication of this manuscript. The authors were concerned for many years that release of this story, closely based on fact, and entirely factual as to the aspects involving MK-ULTRA and psychedelics such as LSD, might place them in professional and perhaps personal jeopardy. Now, enough time has passed – about half a century – to where the authors' misgivings about this publication have considerably (if not entirely) abated.

Foreword

This book is an exposé of what the CIA is capable of doing to its own people and institutions; a unique Princeton love story; an insider exploration of the power and dangers of mind manipulation, hypnosis and psychedelics; and a controversial view of Princeton kids becoming men in the rugged 1960's.

We're currently moving through a strong resurgence of interest in cognitive remodeling, consciousness expansion and psychedelic exploration. This resurgence follows a long period of rejection of mind-chemicals and hypnosis to induce altered states of awareness. After 'The War on Drugs' had effectively shut down LSD research for decades, new scientific research on LSD is now being conducted throughout the world, and Silicon Valley executives openly talk about taking micro-doses of LSD to spur creativity. The founder of Apple even claimed publicly that he would never have come up with his tech breakthroughs without the help of psychedelics.

Blowing America's Mind warps back fifty years to expose some of the very first psychedelic research ever conducted – and shows dramatically just how strange the early years of psychedelic and hypnotic research became. In addition, our account of the untold student culture of all-male Princeton in the late 1960's aims to probe deeper – into a dramatic rendering of the core issue of what consciousness is and how we can manipulate it – for better or for worse.

When first trying to work together to make sense of our Princeton/MK-ULTRA experiences, we felt passionately that this unique Princeton story, and especially the account of our

MK-ULTRA misadventures at the New Jersey Neuro-Psychiatric Institute's Bureau of Research, had to be revealed for public scrutiny. However, our early years of sporadic writing became overwhelmed by a tsunami of books and films all purporting to be the ultimate 1960's story of 'Turn On, Tune In, Drop Out' ... it all blurred into a media-distorted tapestry.

While we were still struggling to make sense of our Princeton experience through writing, the Vietnam War ended and society moved on to new obsessions – computers, wealth accumulation, women's and gay rights, cell phones and the Internet. We always felt, however, that our true story had something important to offer that differed from all the other 1960's material. We aimed to capture what it was really like, from the inside-out, to be caught up in MK-ULTRA's grip.

The New Jersey Neuro-Psychiatric Institute had several aspects. On the one hand, there were incurable psychotic permanent residents in buildings on part of the grounds. However, there was also a Department of Experimental Psychology, which was headed by Humphry Osmond, MD, and Bernard S. Aaronson, Ph.D, the men who co-authored *Psychedelics: The Uses and Implications of Hallucinogenic Drugs*. At this research institute, both LSD and hypnosis were being used to explore altered states of consciousness – but when we became involved, we certainly were never told that we were being used as subjects in the CIA's highly-classified MK-ULTRA mind control project. MK-ULTRA had supposedly ended a few years prior to our misadventures, but later research established that it definitely had not been terminated, and we were two of the guinea pigs.

That news of MK-ULTRA broke for the first time in 1977, almost a decade after our involvement. Headlines blazed about the participation of both Princeton and Columbia University in CIA mind-control research. Media exposure resulted in the overlords at the New Jersey Neuro-Psychiatric Institute being removed from their positions, along with several complicit professors at Princeton University.

However, before this was all exposed, as unwitting college students we underwent a great many hours of deep hypnosis, and also micro-dose LSD sessions, in order to explore the 'outer and inner reaches' of consciousness, from the expanded perceptions of psychedelic euphoria to the dark, demented recesses of schizophrenia. The stated purpose of these studies was to distinguish mind-contracting experiences like schizophrenia and paranoia from mind-expanding perceptions induced by psychedelics. Humphry Osmond's deeper intent was to demonstrate that psychedelics (a term coined by Osmond) did not bring on states of insanity, but rather a sort of temporary super-consciousness.

Needless to say, as young vulnerable students our lives were shaken by participating in such radical research. The idyllic aspects of our Ivy League life were seriously disrupted by our involvement in 'surfing the chaos' as Timothy Leary liked to say.

After graduating, we got together on the west coast and roughed out the first draft of this book. Then we went our separate ways – Paul Jeffrey Davids into the world of television and film in Los Angeles, and John Selby into an adventurous life of travel, research, teaching and writing books. Several times over the years we rewrote our story, but it has never previously been released. We're pleased at this late date to publish this book, without concern for the wounds these old memories may inflict upon Princeton or the CIA – they'll survive the publication of our account. As for our title, we're using part of a 1977 editorial headline from the Los Angeles Times entitled: "The CIA: Blowing America's Mind."

John Selby and Paul Jeffrey Davids
Los Angeles, California / August, 2017

The CIA: Blowing America's Mind

Once again this nation confronts the question of how to prevent its powerful, secret intelligence agencies from becoming a threat to the very freedoms they were established to protect from internal and external enemies.

The latest revelations show that the Central Intelligence Agency's drug-experimentation program was far more extensive than the agency ever admitted before, and was one that may have been discontinued only recently.

Documents forced from the agency under the Freedom of Information Act reveal that CIA conducted a secret, 25-year project in which mind-altering drugs were tested on human beings to gauge the drugs' ability to disturb memory, change sex patterns and create aberrational response.

The documents further disclose that:

—The CIA involved 185 researchers and 80 institutions in the experiments; most of the researchers and some of the institutions were unaware that they were being used by the agency.

—The CIA established whorehouses in San Francisco and New York that were used for experiments with LSD and other potent drugs; prostitutes gave the drugs to unwitting subjects.

—Some testing was carried out on unwitting subjects in a ward for criminal sexual psychopaths in a state hospital.

—Similar experiments were conducted on prison inmates said to have consented to the tests.

How much injury may have been caused to unwitting human targets can only be guessed at, but an earlier congressional investigation revealed that an Army scientist, who had been given LSD without his knowledge, committed suicide.

The experiments began out of concern in the 1950s that the Russians and the Chinese had developed effective techniques in mind control, and that these techniques might be used to control the minds of American prisoners of war or American diplomats.

But somewhere along the line, CIA Director Stansfield Turner told a congressional committee, the CIA project changed in character from defensive to offensive.

That should have been no surprise. For the past quarter-century, our intelligence community has been permitted by a lax Congress and a succession of Presidents to become virtually a secret government. Power unchecked is power that will be abused, and the secret exercise of authority, without strict controls, magnifies the danger.

The Los Angeles Times, August 1977 Editorial

Research Report 1971

BUREAU OF RESEARCH IN NEUROLOGY AND PSYCHIATRY

NEW JERSEY NEURO-PSYCHIATRIC INSTITUTE

NEW JERSEY MENTAL HEALTH RESEARCH AND DEVELOPMENT FUND

SKILLMAN, NEW JERSEY

Nassau Hall, site of the office of the President, Princeton University

Table of Contents

1. Music for Zen Love

Jonathan was lying in the reclining hypnosis chair in Bernie Aaronson's office with his eyes closed, his breathing deep and slow, his mind alert to the sounds coming through the walls from other rooms in the building ... voices talking in the distance, typewriters clacking away, someone playing 'Lucy in the Sky with Diamonds' from the Beatles' new album 'Sgt. Pepper's Lonely Hearts Club Band.'

Bernie's hypnotic suggestions from five minutes ago were still lingering in Jonathan's mind. "Let yourself relax now, Jonathan ... and allow absolutely everything we've done today to sink into the great white fog of forgetfulness forever. Just tune into your physical senses in the present moment ... expand your awareness to include yourself and everything around you ... and in five minutes or so you can slowly begin to rise up into waking consciousness and carry on with your day back at Princeton."

In his deep-trance condition Jonathan had heard the sound of Bernie standing up and walking over to him, and had felt him giving him the ritual parting kiss on the forehead. The sensation of Bernie's wet lips on his skin had made Jonathan tense – but nothing else had happened. Bernie's footsteps went walking out the door and on down the hallway – the nasty smell of his cigarette smoke still in the air.

Time passed. Jonathan's heart kept on beating in a natural rhythm, his inhales and exhales flowing all on their own, empowered by some blissful invisible inflow of energy. Then without his willing them to open, his eyelids lifted and his eyes came alive.

The visual reality of Bernie's messy office was a shock. Jonathan wanted to close his eyes again and just drift off into infinite amniotic spaces forever. However, something down in his misty fog zones was reminding him that he was supposed to get up from the reclining chair. Yes, he definitely wanted to head back to campus to indulge in some weekend fun and get away from Bernie's subversive universe … at least until Monday.

He pulled the wooden lever, sat upright in the chair and for a tense, confused moment tried to remember what exactly had happened to him during the last hour – but Bernie had told him as usual that what had happened was now forever lost in thick impenetrable fog. There was now only Bernie's desk, his swivel chair, his worn Persian rug and his set of locked file cabinets.

The sight of those file cabinets struck Jonathan with a negative jolt. He felt his chest tense, his breaths tighten as an old cowboy tendency he'd picked up from his dad erupted – the reflex to distrust everybody. Bernie had been helping him for almost two years now to let go of those ingrained defensive habits and open up. Still –

Jonathan felt a compulsion to go over and see if the file cabinets were unlocked. He knew that all of the hypnotic conditions that Bernie had given him during the research sessions were recorded somewhere, probably in one of those drawers. Also there would be the secret results of Bernie's off-the-record LSD experiments he'd been undertaking with Dr. Humphry Osmond's blessing – giving subjects micro-doses of acid, around 30 mics per hypnotic session. Jonathan wanted to know the results of those studies, and also who'd funded them.

But when he pulled at the drawers he found every one of them locked up tight. Suddenly fast footsteps were coming down the hall outside the office. Jonathan spun around, afraid of getting caught in the act. Luckily, the footsteps continued on their way along the hall.

He opened the door to Bernie's office and walked quickly down the old corridor, his worn-out cowboy boots making a racket on the linoleum floor. Downstairs when he nodded goodbye to pretty Linda at the front desk, she shouted something at his back as he went out the door. He didn't go back in to see what she'd said – they'd gone a romantic round together last month and she'd given him her all, but it somehow hadn't been the 'all' he was still hungering for.

Down at the parking lot he jumped into his MG with the top down, fired up the ancient engine, popped the clutch and roared out of the parking lot. The Institute's three-story red brick building was a couple hundred yards away from the main buildings of the New Jersey Neuro-Psychiatric Institute where patients were housed. A narrow lake ran alongside the long driveway to the county road, and Jonathan's eyes happened to catch a bright glint of late afternoon sunlight reflecting off the surface of the narrow lake beside the long drive – and suddenly he was remembering back six months ago, being with Bernie down there by the water during a hypnotic condition, with Bernie telling him the lake was freezing over, even though it was spring and a warm day.

The memory suddenly vanished as Jonathan drove fast out onto the country road heading toward Princeton. The first tight curve at the top of the hill was one of his favorites, and he took it at max torque, downshifting at just the right second, totally absorbed in the power-on sensation rush. The present moment was definitely the only place to live, just like Humphry and Bernie were always saying – stay continually focused on the very center of God's universe, tap the secret of Zen.

But several curves later, his mind drifting again into that lake-turned-to-ice flashback, Jonathan was two seconds late in downshifting and almost slid off the road. Damn, he wasn't supposed to remember any of those conditions Bernie had given him –

It was early in the fall semester of 1967. Princeton was six miles and about six thousand light years from the Institute. The ancient sprawling well-pruned campus out in the hinterlands of New Jersey was such a safe conservative place compared with the Institute. And weekends at Princeton meant girls – sure this was the university of F. Scott Fitzgerald and Albert Einstein, Woodrow Wilson and Adlai Stevenson, Ralph Nader and Jimmy Stewart, and the ghosts of those hallowed greats still hovered over every square inch of the campus. The only trouble with the place was that it was still an all-male school. There was talk that maybe Princeton would go coed in a couple years, maybe in the autumn of 1969, but Jonathan would be gone by then and it wouldn't help his current situation at all.

Today was Friday and there was no fencing meet this weekend. Jonathan sat a moment in the parking lot practicing a new meditation technique – but his faltering desire for monastic enlightenment kept getting overpowered by an overt hunger for female companionship.

He unbent himself from the MG and walked across campus eyeing early female arrivals from various women's colleges who were out strolling with their proud Princeton dates. Jonathan reflexively and mostly subliminally imagined what the experience might be to get intimate with each girl he passed – slipping into high school fantasy games as he made his way to his dormitory in Little Hall.

The massive old building looked like a medieval castle – four stories of stone walls and small lead-glass windows. He opened the heavy outside door just as Glen Murphy, a friend from the first-floor suite, came running down the stairs dressed in party coat and tie.

"Hey, Jonathan, there you are – have you decided yet?"

"Uhm, oh, I forgot about your party – who's Rachael bringing?"

"Her roommate from N.Y.U. and some girl from Columbia, and some chick visiting from California. How about showing up this time?"

"So who gets who?"

"That'll just have to work itself out."

Jonathan grinned, doing his best to play gung-ho. "Well what the hell, one more blind date won't kill me."

Glen smiled a pleased look, slapped Jonathan on the back in traditional Princeton-Charlie style, and went running off on his manic errand to buy more rubbers or more gin or who knows what else for the party. Jonathan headed up the interior stone stairs. It was a long way to his dorm hideaway at the top of the building, but he liked the seclusion – the feeling of living in the bird's nest – and it was good training for fencing to run up and down so many stairs every day.

When he opened his door and went into his one-room monk's space, he found the tall narrow window open. His friend Pok must have come by. He closed the window, turned up his radiator and wondered what sort of girl he might meet tonight. His lingering cowboy dreams still hoped that the woman of his life would just suddenly appear out of the blue and make him feel whole, transforming his solitary life like his mom had done for his dad.

In the last couple years his romances had blown up in his face over and over again. East Coast girls seemed almost like a different species compared to the girls he'd known back home. But what the hell – he pushed choked-up romantic thoughts out of mind and put on 'Sergeant Pepper' for perhaps the fiftieth time. He hoped that Pok would show up to gab and maybe smoke a bit – but glancing at his watch, he realized that if he didn't go down and shower away the karmic dust from his day at the Institute, he might not even get within touching distance of a clean-scrubbed blind-date dream-girl.

Hot pounding water, wet tiles and blissful steam took the tension out of his shoulder muscles. Soft intimations of a night of making love came over him as he relaxed and lathered himself all over, getting got caught up in a hard sexual passion to finally slide into a really intimate relationship with a girl – sharing the really deep stuff in his life like what was going on at the Institute –

Suddenly he felt a pain in his stomach as nausea wiped out every trace of his sexual fantasy. He turned off the water and stood there holding his stomach, thinking gnarly flu thoughts – but the pain was easing now. As the nausea subsided, Jonathan just barely caught a sense of Bernie's presence right where the pain had been. The juxtaposed feelings of pain and some sort of hypnotic condition made Jonathan's knees weak, and when he tried to reflect on the connection between the two, the nausea started again –

Rick Warren, another classmate who lived in the same dorm wing, came bursting into the bathroom and found Jonathan standing there immobile, eyes vacant, pain on his face.

"Jonathan, are you all right, what's the matter?"

"Uhm."

"What's going on, are you on drugs or something?"

Emerging somewhat from the strange feelings, Jonathan shrugged. "I was just remembering my last blind date."

"You looked really pale, as if you were in a trance."

"You're the philosophy major, you know that everything's a trance," Jonathan countered to defend himself. "How about the state of mind you're in right now?"

"Maybe you should go to the infirmary."

"Rick, relax, I'm okay."

"Your friend Pok was looking for you."

Rick always mispronounced Pok's name, calling him 'Poke,' as in 'a poke in the ribs.' The correct way to say it was 'Pock,' as in 'he's got a joint in his pocket' – a condition that was almost always true about Pok.

"What did he want?"

"You know that guy, mumbling things I could hardly understand. All that hypnosis stuff messed up his mind, he was perfectly okay before he started working out there at that Institute. And we're worried about you too – you've changed this year, Jonathan, it seems like you've lost contact with us."

Jonathan shrugged, bothered by the comment. "Hey, aren't we having a party tonight, just like in the good old days? How about you jump in the shower and lather up your big ol' wong for the girls."

Upstairs, feeling hot after the shower, Jonathan opened his tall narrow window and stepped naked out onto the stone ledge high above the campus. Back on the ranch there'd been a cliff he'd ride his horse up to when he needed to get centered … now he stood silent for twelve breaths, eyes closed, feeling good again in his belly – then he opened his eyes to take in the truly lovely, mystic, magical aura of Princeton as it came alive on a Friday eve with three thousand lonely guys like himself, absolutely craving even the slightest touch of a visiting angel of the night ...

He put on Levi's and a blue workshirt and pulled on his elkhide boots. He'd given up a lot now that he was off the ranch and trying to act Ivy League cool, but he still mostly stuck with his cowboy clothes. His dad had told him that as long as he didn't dress the way city people did, he wouldn't start thinking like them. If it had been up to his dad, Jonathan wouldn't have left the ranch and come East to college – his dad claimed that spending money on college was like pouring good whiskey down a gopher hole. His mom, who'd in fact gone to college, had felt otherwise – but she was long gone.

He buttoned up his shirt and headed down to the living room in the suite below. "Jonathan, there you are," Glen intoned, eyeing Jonathan's proletariat shirt disdainfully. "Come meet the girls."

Jonathan stood outwardly calm, watching his breathing while Glen went through the introductions. He'd already met Glen's girlfriend Rachael. They made a good pair, for sure – Glen liked big boobs and she had big boobs – no, that wasn't fair, he thought to himself – but at the same time it was accurate. And her two roommates from New York – one of them had a good figure but was looking at Jonathan like he was too freaky even to talk to, and the other was sort of frail and mousy, and besides, Rick was interested in her and the last thing in the world Jonathan wanted to do, since he liked Rick, was to foul up Rick's romance.

"And this is our guest, an artist from San Francisco," Glen said. "Gee, I'm sorry, I've forgotten your name."

"Anne," she said quietly, nodding her head just slightly in Jonathan's direction.

"Howdy," Jonathan said. Looking deeply into her eyes, he somewhat bashfully returned her smile – and then everybody sat back in chairs and sofas. Glen finished preparing drinks; Jonathan succumbed to gin of British origin splashed over ice.

Gin out of the bottle had almost killed him his sophomore year, he'd been down in two feet of snow after midnight on his way back to his dorm and if a proctor hadn't miraculously come by, Jonathan probably would have departed the scene right then, warm in snow, end of story.

To Jonathan's acute ears, the ensuing sub-harmonious din of random conversation suddenly sounded quite a bit like feeding time down at the hen-house –he'd been in charge of a couple dozen chickens as a kid and, as he sat on a bar stool, he once again felt hopelessly left out of Princeton's party buzz –

He let his focus return to the girl from San Francisco who was now nestled comfortably across the room in an arm-chair, looking out the window. She glanced down at her glass and then looked directly at him and caught him looking at her soft blue sweater; short skirt, knitted wool, no nylons –

He kicked his perennially bashful butt off the barstool and went over to sit down on the window-seat beside her. Like his literary hero Richard Farina once wrote, 'nothing ventured, nothing gained – and nothing still remains.'

"So how long have you been out from Seattle?"

"San Francisco. Two weeks." She had a low voice, soft and resonant. He liked it.

"And what're you doing in New York?"

"I was ready to get away from home. I thought maybe New York would be inspiring."

"So you're an artist. You paint?"

"I do. These days, I'm mainly painting horses."

"Not many horses in New York."

"I spent several days at the Remington exhibit at the Met," she said. "His horses are incredible."

"Yeah – I used to be really into horses too, back home. I had three while I was growing up – not for pleasure, it was all work. I agree with you, horses are, yeah, just that – incredible. But that's all past tense."

Her eyes held his gaze. "Why is that?"

"Uhm, I'm not exactly welcome on the ranch these days," he admitted.

"Do you want to tell me why?"

"Something about my not being a gung-ho Christian willing to go fight in Vietnam and things like that – but hey, my big brother went to 'Nam and came back a total disaster." Jonathan fell silent for a moment and then went on, his voice tense and low. "Well actually, what happened was my Dad phoned me one night about a week after that big scare-article on LSD came out in Time Magazine."

"Yes, I read it."

"He said he just wanted to warn me against getting near any of that dangerous brain-damaging stuff. Without thinking I told him, being acutely honest at the time, that he was about three days too late. He hung up the phone with a curse and he hasn't talked to me since."

"You don't even go home for holidays?"

"Not anymore."

The party was getting underway with the Supremes on the stereo turned up full blast. More people were showing up and Jonathan was starting to feel uncomfortable like he always did at parties. "Want another drink?" he asked the California girl.

"I'm not much of a drinker," she responded evenly.

"Me neither. But at parties –"

"You don't have to apologize. Go on, help yourself."

So he went to get himself another drink. The first one had taken the edge off his nervousness, maybe the second would get him into full party gear. He wished he'd taken a puff before the party but Pok hadn't replenished his supply. Grass definitely relieved social uptightness.

When he returned his heart skipped a beat – she was nowhere in sight. He went out onto the large living room balcony in search of her and there she was, standing alone in the night air looking down on the scene below – lamplight and the scented grassy smell of evening mist, sounds of party music from all over the campus wafting in through the vacuum of the night.

"So you like Princeton?" he said, leaning against the low stone wall that kept drunken bodies from careening down three floors.

"It's physically beautiful," she said simply, looking at two paths down below filled with half-drunk aristocrats' grandsons walking beside their Smith and Vassar dates – lingering traces of the long-gone F. Scott Fitzgerald era that still haunted the campus after all these years.

"Einstein was a prof here," Jonathan said. "Sometimes it seems his spirit still hovers around, getting into my dreams, telling me not to take any of this seriously – everything's relative and all that."

He stopped himself, feeling slightly intoxicated and jabbering nonsense.

"Wayne told me you do work in hypnosis," Anne said.

"Well, I just finished as a hypnotic subject. I might get promoted to staff hypnotist next week."

"I know a psychiatrist in Mill Valley, a good friend of my father – he started using hypnotherapy but then stopped. He said it violated the free will of his clients."

"Not at all necessarily. Hypnosis is just an extreme form of how we relate all the time," Jonathan explained a bit defensively. "When I say to you, imagine a red rose, and in your mind's eye you imagine a red rose, you've taken a suggestion from me – and that's hypnosis. When we really listen and respond to each other we're engaging in suggestibility, in mutual hypnosis. Hey, it's getting real noisy."

"Yeah, the music is pretty deafening. It's getting hard for me to hear you."

"Would you like to go up to my room, put on some quieter music?"

She nodded.

They walked back into the living room, dodging drunken bodies on the dance floor and stepping over the early casualties. Glen stopped gyrating long enough to pull Jonathan to one side. "Come on, get out here and show Anne your cowboy stomp," he shouted over the sound of Mick Jagger belting out 'Let's Spend the Night Together.'

"I'm bushed, we're going up to my room," Jonathan said, with Anne standing close beside him.

Glen gave her the 'ah-ha!' eye, elbowed Jonathan, said "Atta boy!" and returned to his dancing.

She was light on her feet following him up the steep attic stairs. As they entered his room, she paused to take in the Persian material hanging on the ceiling like a sheik's tent, and the six foot wide, two-foot high canvas on the wall depicting the world's first psychedelic interpretation of the Mona Lisa – a giant abstract pair of puckered lips.

"My best friend Pok, he painted that," said Jonathan. "If he'd just put himself into it he could really go places."

"What did you say his name is?"

"Pok. It's short for his real name, Apokalos."

"What kind of a name is that?"

"Half American Indian, half Greek. We roomed together freshman and sophomore years."

She sat down cross-legged on a throw pillow on the rug, hands in her lap. Jonathan went over to his record collection and pulled out an album. "You like classical music?" he said.

"Very much."

"What kind?"

"Most of it up until Mahler."

He put on Brahms's Second Piano Concerto, his mother's favorite. French horns stated the theme of the first movement.

"Is that the Sviataslav Richter recording," she asked.

He smiled, met her eyes again. "You got that right."

The full orchestra suddenly grew silent as the pianist went into a complex solo, delicate yet powerful. Anne swayed to the music. Jonathan went over to sit on his bed where he could get maximum stereo separation. Anne glanced over at him, a little unsure of what to do, so he suggested that she come sit beside him where she could get maximum stereo separation too.

They listened to the entire first movement without speaking. When the second movement began, she broke the silence. "Can I hear more about the hypnosis?" she asked.

"Like what?"

"I don't care. It just interests me."

"Well our research out at the New Jersey Neuro-Psychiatric Institute is sponsored by the National Institute of Mental Health, part of NIH. We use the trance state to induce all kinds of altered awareness, including mystical states, even temporary nirvana."

"No, sorry – you can't just hypnotize someone and have them attain enlightenment."

"Well last year, Dr. Humphry Osmond, who runs the place, recorded the EEG readings, you know, brainwave stuff, of three Zen monks in meditation and identified their brain patterns – it's mostly a particular segment of alpha, and the same alpha patterns can be induced through a particular hypnosis condition. The procedure isn't perfected yet, but –"

"Are you telling me that you've been hypnotized and actually attained nirvana?"

"Well, it's hard to say. We get post-hypnotic conditions after each session to erase our memory of what happened."

"They erase your memory?"

"Just of the hypnotic condition."

"Why did you let them do that?"

"It's part of the research paradigm that Bernie and Dr. Osmond developed. Bernie Aaronson is the psychologist I work under at the Institute – he's my hypnotist, actually. Bernie is in charge of the hypnosis program, and Humphrey Osmond is the psychiatrist who is head of the entire Bureau of Research. From what I hear, the Institute was set up mostly by the Kennedy family through NIH – Bobby Kennedy took LSD twice out there, guided by Dr. Osmond – but as Bernie tells it, Lyndon Johnson's daughter freaked out on acid in the White House one night and Johnson immediately shut down all seven federal LSD research centers – so we supposedly had to shift to using hypnosis to induce the same states. Between you and me, Humphry and Bernie still have plenty of high quality Sandoz acid that was never turned in, and sure, occasionally we use an off-the-record assist from psychedelics. That's a term that Dr. Osmond invented – it means 'mind manifesting.' Dr. Osmond guided Aldous Huxley on Huxley's first trip with mescaline – Huxley wrote a whole book about it, *The Doors of Perception.*"

"My brother read that book," said Anne. "But I'd be afraid to let anyone or any drug tamper with my mind. I mean, it's definitely interesting. I love psychology, my father's a psychologist – but psychedelic drugs sound like a freaky thing to get into. A friend took me down to Haight Ashbury one night and somehow it didn't appeal to me – too many vacant stares and scared girls. I don't think anybody could hypnotize me – they say some people can't be hypnotized."

"Everyone's susceptible, some people just take longer to go under. You want me to show you?"

"How do I know you're not out to control me?"

"Why would I want to do that?"

"Why hypnotize somebody other than to control them?"

"Hypnosis just helps you get into a state you'd attain anyway if you meditated for ten years. It's a tool, a shortcut."

"So then, what do I have to do?" she said.

"Just lay down on my bed on your back."

She smiled. "Ah, the old line."

He smiled back. It did sound like 'the old line' when he thought about it. But in this case, nothing was farther from the truth. "You don't trust me?" he asked.

"Well, are you trustworthy?"

"I do my best."

"Alright then." She made a graceful move with her whole body and stretched herself out on the bed. Jonathan turned off the music and pulled up a chair beside her. She smoothed out her skirt and crossed her bare legs.

He could feel himself getting excited in spite of himself. Hey, down boy, he ordered. "Okay now, just close your eyes, let yourself feel the softness of the bed ... begin to relax all the muscles in your body ... first your feet, your knees, your pelvis, your arms and hands, your throat, your tongue, your jaw, and your eyes. I'll just take you down a little bit this time, just breathe deeply, that's good. Feel yourself inhaling, exhaling, your body relaxing ... go ahead and feel a warm soothing sensation of total peace coming into your whole being ..."

Her eyes closed and she stretched her entire body, slowly and sensually like a cat. Her sweater was pulled tight across her breasts. No bra.

"Focus completely on your breathing now, just watch as the air comes into your lungs, then flows out without any effort – in . . . out . . . in . . . out . . ."

She stretched again and he had the sudden urge to bend over her, feel her, kiss her lips – anything to relieve the pressure that was building inside him. But – right then a pang of nausea hit him in the gut. He managed to continue talking, but mostly on automatic.

"Enjoy that peaceful, drifting, soft warm state of mind and body, spirit, soul … you're just quietly listening to my words, letting your thoughts drift far away ... you can trust me now to take you deeper and deeper, so that my voice becomes your voice, and whatever suggestions I make seem to be suggestions coming from your own mind."

Her eyes blinked open. "I don't want your voice taking me over like that," she muttered.

"But –"

She was now sitting up on the bed. "I'm sorry, Jonathan, I just don't believe in letting someone else direct my thoughts. I shouldn't have started this, I knew I wouldn't be open to it." She made a move, stood up. "Can I put on another record?"

"Uhm, sure."

She went over to the record collection, knelt down and started fingering through the albums – took out a record and put it on. The needle settled in the groove, and they heard the sound of a soft Japanese wooden flute, soft like an evening dove. Then the 4-string koto was weaving in and out of the modal tune, the vibrating strings perfectly in harmony with the flute. 'Music for Zen Meditation,' the best record in his collection. She came over and sat down again next to him on the bed. "Okay?" she asked of the music.

"Definitely. Alan Watts, a spiritual teacher and writer who lives in California but sometimes comes out to the Institute –

he set up the recording of that album over in Tokyo. He's great. He wrote an incredible book called *Psychotherapy East and West.*"

"Oh?"

"He came by the Institute last month for a party and I was just, well, really deeply struck by him – to know someone my dad's age who's so different from my dad. I want to do graduate studies in San Francisco with him – but the draft, you know – to stay out of the Army I need the deferment that I'll get from the Institute." Jonathan paused and took a breath. He realized he'd been rapping quite a bit. "But enough about me, what about your parents, your dad – I've done most of the talking so far."

"Well – what you see is what you get," she said a bit defensively. "My father was a musician but when I was little he shifted into psychology – he teaches at Marin College. My mom died when I was eleven -- that was really harsh. Ah, right now I'm feeling so relaxed, I did like the hypnosis. I'd rather listen to this music than chatter. I don't know much about meditation but I do love that flute."

She closed her eyes and left Jonathan feeling in awe, thankful to be with this particular girl all alone, she seemed to be physically radiating warm exciting energy ... he gazed at her face and then down to her breasts and on down to her bare legs and then up again to her lips – and again wanted more than anything to give in to his impulse to kiss her, to surrender to his urge. But instead, being a shy cowboy at heart, he closed his own eyes and focused on his breathing.

Inhale, exhale. Inhale, exhale ... down boy. He could hear her breathing right beside him and paced his breathing with hers, everything slowing down, becoming altered, lightened. He felt his body starting to float upward ... ah yes, that hypnotic condition to experience weightlessness, zero gravity, the feeling of levitation – he was experiencing it again for no reason at all, just like that day with Bernie when he was told to float up six inches off the hypnosis chair. It had seemed completely real then – and now it was happening again ...

A hot burning energy sensation started rushing up his spine from his lower chakras. He felt naked and exposed and vulnerable in the extreme – his eyes popped open on their own and he found Anne looking right at him with a soft smile on her lips, just like the smile on the wall in Pok's painting. He met her gaze and the adrenaline hit his groin and his heart started pumping like crazy and his lips started moving toward her and she was leaning toward him and then somebody banged on the door and scared them both shitless.

"Anne, are you in there?" It was Rachael, shouting. "Come on, it's time to go, we're going to miss the last bus. What're you doing in there anyway?"

Anne sighed. She smiled. "We're busted," she whispered. "Perhaps just as well, I was getting, well – overheated."

She stood up. Jonathan stood up with her and they faced each other, standing very close. He could feel her warm breath on his skin. "I think I really like you, Jonathan. Phone me, okay? Glen has my number."

She stood on her tiptoes, kissed him on the mouth, squeezed his hand – and then went quickly out through the door, closing it gently behind her.

He sat back down on his bed. He could still smell her slight fragrance. And he could still see that special lovely look in her eyes – but right in the middle of his euphoria, once again he got hit with that pang of nausea – and the whole bubble collapsed.

D12M

THE NEW YORK TIMES, FRIDAY, AUGUST 26, 1977

C.I.A. Tells Columbia, Princeton Of Secret Behavioral Research

By JOSEPH B. TREASTER

The Central Intelligence Agency has informed Columbia and Princetown Universities that they are among 86 institutions where secret research is believed to have ben conducted in an attempt by the agency to develop ways to manipulate the behavior of human beings, spokesmen for the universities said on Wednesday.

The agency did not indicate what kinds of experiments were carried out at the universities, when they were done and who participated, the spokesmen said. Nor, they said, did the agency indicate whether the experiments resulted in deaths or injuries.

A team of New York Times reporters disclosed the scope and general outline of the C.I.A.'s investigations into behavior and thought control, ranging over 25 years and costing some $25 million, in articles published on Aug. 2 and 3.

At a Senate hearing on Aug. 3, Adm. Stansfield Turner, the director of Central Intelligence, gave additional details, including the fact that 86 institutions were involved. He said the agency had financed the work of 185 nongovernment researchers at these institutions—universities, hospitals, prisons and pharmaceutical companies—on 149 separate research projects.

Admiral Turner said a few days after the hearing that the C.I.A. would notify the institutions that appeared to have been involved in the program, but that they would have to decide whether they wanted their roles made public.

In recent days officials at several academic institutions have acknowledged to inquiring reporters that they were involved in the experiments. Among them are the Unversity of Pennsylvania, Ohio State University, George Washington University and the University of Maryland. The Times had previously independently confirmed that the C.I.A. had planned to test drugs on terminal cancer patients at the Georgetown University Medical School.

Columbia and Princeton were notified in letters last week, the spokesmen said, that they had apparently been involved in a phase of C.I.A. testing between 1953 and 1964.

The letters said the universities had been among "the institutions at which some portion of the research appears to have been performed, or with which one or more individuals performing some aspect of it were affiliated."

Spokesmen for Columbia and Princeton said the universities were "looking into the matter" and had requested additional information from the C.I.A.

Jonathan on horseback at his family's ranch in Ojai, California

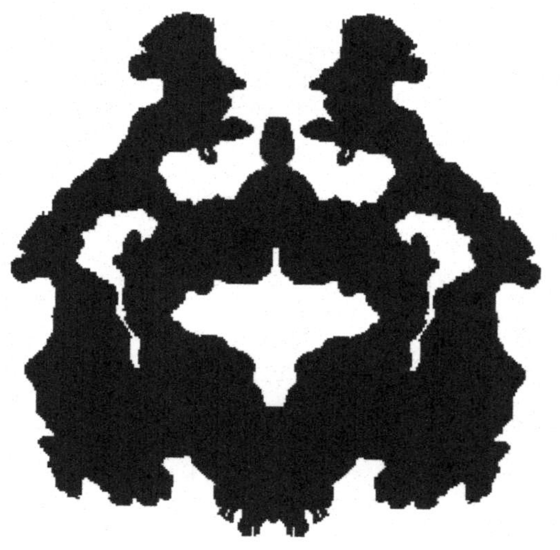

A Rorschach Inkblot

2. Rorschach Inkblots

Paul J. Davids, called by his middle name, Jeffrey, by most of his sophomore buddies at Princeton, was cooped up in a small room on the second floor of a large brick building that seemed as though it might have once been somebody's private estate. He kept glancing out the window, feeling distracted as he struggled with a battery of questionnaires, divulging his likes, dislikes, habits, aims, preferences, ideals and opinions.

The window looked out on the expanse of acreage of the Institute grounds and a long, inviting lake. It was a much more beautiful environment than he'd expected when he decided a few days before to apply to be a deep hypnosis subject. Then again, he hadn't known what to expect.

The inside of the building was cozy but old and sort of dusty, and most of the walls seemed to need a fresh coat of paint. The hardwood floors had lost their shine long ago and creaked. He could even make the floor creak right now, just by pushing down with his foot.

He tried to concentrate once again on the questionnaire. Did he like sweets? Sure. He could stuff himself with chocolate, ice cream and popsicles. What did he think of long hair? On girls it was fine. Was the United Nations a viable force for creating peace in the world? With the war still raging in Vietnam, it obviously wasn't doing too stellar a job. So should he answer 'no' or 'sometimes?' His head was swimming in circles.

He even had to write an essay about what he thought of life at Princeton. Jeffrey had nothing but respect for the university, but it was hard to ignore the fact that there were 3,500 male undergraduates and zero females, a fact that contributed to all sorts of unspeakable pressures in the groin. If he'd known it was going to be so hard to meet girls, he probably would have gone to a college with a more plentiful surrounding of bountiful bosoms.

Of course, he wasn't about to admit that in his essay, which he filled with platitudes and clichés. Then Mike Kerner, the bearded young psychologist administering the tests, had him write another essay on why he wanted to be a hypnotic subject. That was hard to answer honestly. On the one hand, he usually felt uptight whenever the opportunity came up to ask a girl for a date (which wasn't all that often), and it seemed logical that hypnosis might teach him to relax. Possibly improve his sex life. He wasn't too keen on remaining a virgin much longer. But there were other things influencing him, too, and some of it had to do with the claims of Dr. Timothy Leary, the former Harvard psychology professor who proclaimed the virtues of LSD and other psychedelic drugs and what Dr. Leary called expanded consciousness. Jeffrey had read Dr. Leary's claims in a lengthy interview in Playboy, and he had a natural curiosity about all of that – LSD as the ultimate aphrodisiac that puts you in touch with the hidden intelligence that supposedly is dormant in billions of cells of your brain that aren't used in everyday waking consciousness. His curiosity was raised all the more when he learned that actor Cary Grant also extolled the benefits of LSD as a form of psychotherapy.

Jeffrey had heard rumors that some of the hypnosis subjects at the New Jersey Neuro-Psychiatric Institute were given the opportunity to try LSD under clinical conditions. He wasn't sure where he first heard those rumors. Probably it was informal talk over at the Psychology Department building, and he was planning on majoring in Psychology. In any event, he figured, why not begin at the Institute by trying hypnosis, and maybe other opportunities for exotic mind experiences would flow from there.

To help him write the second essay, Jeffrey took a flyer from his shirt pocket and unfolded it to read it again:

N. J. NEURO-PSYCHIATRIC INSTITUTE

Subjects Needed for Deep Hypnosis Experiments

The Bureau of Research in Neurology and Psychiatry of the New Jersey Neuro-Psychiatric Institute needs subjects willing to undergo deep hypnosis. Subjects will be paid during an initial training period and then will participate in a series of experiments. You must be willing to make a long-term commitment. If accepted, you will undergo hypnosis several times a week and may make an important contribution to our understanding of human consciousness.

Mike, who was smoking up the room with his pipe, was scoring the Rorschach Inkblot Personality Test he had administered to Jeffrey earlier. Finally Jeffrey handed in his two finished essays. Mike glanced at them while Jeffrey tried his best to act at ease.

Mike put the essays aside and filled his pipe again from the tobacco tin on the desk. "Tell me, Jeffrey, did taking these tests make you at all nervous?"

"Nervous?" Jeffrey felt a lump in his throat. "No, I don't think so."

"You came out a bit defensive," Mike said, looking at him seriously through his wire-rimmed glasses.

"Really?" Disaster.

"I thought maybe you'd just been a little nervous. It doesn't necessarily mean anything serious."

"Oh. Well, maybe I was just a little. Nervous, that is. I mean, a little bit nervous."

"Why don't we run through the Rorschach again?"

"Okay, great."

Jeffrey wondered how he could possibly have come out as defensive. He'd planned all his answers carefully to be as academic and coherent as possible. He'd kept nothing back and had been open – except for his failure to mention his hope that hypnosis might help improve his sexual batting average.

As Mike reshuffled the Rorschach inkblot cards, Jeffrey tried to collect himself and figure out a new approach.

"Okay now," Mike began, holding up the first card, "What do you see in this one, Jeffrey?"

"You want the first thing that comes into my head?"

"Exactly."

The last time, Jeffrey had said that he saw a butterfly in the inkblot. He could still distinctly make out the two wings and the body. "Well, those roundish blobs, I'm not sure. A woman's breasts, probably. And the line in the middle – a vagina."

Mike raised his eyebrows and went on to the next inkblot.

That time, Jeffrey passed with flying colors.

"Why don't you go down to the library on the first floor and look through some books?" said Mike. "I'll call you up to see Bernie after I've had a few words with him."

"Okay. I can't wait to meet Dr. Aaronson."

"By the way, when you meet him, don't be so formal. Call him Bernie. Just Bernie."

"Bernie. Got it."

The library was fantastic. Every kind of weird esoteric book you could possibly imagine was on those shelves. There were volumes on the psychological ramifications of shrunken heads, on cannibal tribal cultures. There was an encyclopedia of sexual fantasies, and books on out-of-the-body experiences, astral projection, necrophilia, schizophrenia, paranoia, communication from beyond the grave, witchcraft, the history of E.S.P. and the maladjustment of teenagers in contemporary society.

By contrast, the psychology library back at Princeton was dullsville. All they seemed to stock there were books on albino rats – Rat Child Development, Rat Interpersonal Relations, Rat Religion, Rat Psychopathology and Rat Neuropsychiatry. It was part of the prevailing 'B. F. Skinner approach' that thrived in psychology departments throughout the Ivy League, which put the study of rats in mazes ahead of the study of human personality. It was enough to make Jeffrey think that the psych professors at Princeton had a rat fixation.

He heard someone giggling out in the hallway. He poked his head through the library door. A girl was sitting at a desk in the hall, reading a book. She was very attractive, with long, flowing black hair and dark eyes and wearing a low-cut dress. On her cheek she'd drawn a little flower, like the girls out in San Francisco that Jeffrey had read about in Playboy. 'America's Flower Children' had been the title of that article. Apparently college kids from all over the country had flown, motorcycled, even hitch-hiked to San Francisco last summer to go to the love-ins, rock concerts and all the other psychedelic happenings that had gone on out there. Everybody'd had really exciting adventures smoking marijuana and taking trips on LSD, making love with everyone and in general having an exceptional time. Playboy had shown color photographs of exotic hippie girls running naked through the park, skinny-dipping in the ocean and lying around casually with hip-looking guys.

"Well," said the girl at the desk, offering Jeffrey a very friendly smile. "There you are, I thought you were never going to come out of there. I'm Linda Hodges – Bernie Aaronson's assistant. How did your testing go?"

"I don't know yet. Mike said I should wait in the library."

"Well then you can keep me company. Those are really nice pants."

"Thanks. My Mom bought them for me."

"Really?"

"She buys all my clothes."

It was true. And if his mother was still selecting his clothes when he turned thirty, he'd probably sneak out and buy a belt to hang himself. Clothes were something that always had to have the parental stamp of approval in his family, just like movies you went to see (horror films were outlawed) or girls you dated (preferably nice and Jewish).

"You want to see what I did to myself this morning?" said Linda. "It's really horrible."

She swiveled around on her chair and showed him a round bruise on her thigh. It was about the closest he'd ever gotten to a live thigh on a fantastic girl before.

"Boy, you really got a bad bruise there," he said.

"Last night I was doing my yoga – I always do it in the nude, that's the best way – and when I came down from my headstand I banged myself against the corner of my waterbed."

"You've got a waterbed? Wow. I was reading about them in the last issue of Playboy –"

"God, Jeffrey, I hope you're not one of those guys who has Playboy on the brain –"

The intercom buzzed. Jeffrey was wanted upstairs.

Mike was noncommittal as he led Jeffrey through the outer office and into Dr. Aaronson's inner office. Jeffrey couldn't tell whether he'd passed or failed. Mike introduced him to Dr. Aaronson and then made a quick exit.

"So you want to be a hypnotic subject, do you?" Dr. Aaronson said, looking at Jeffrey with an intense stare. "Sit down, make yourself at home and we'll have a little chat."

"Thank you, Dr. Aaronson."

"Please, call me Bernie."

"Oh. Sorry, Dr. Aaronson. I mean, sorry, Bernie."

Bernie lit up a cigarette and took a deep drag on it.

Jeffrey sat down on one of the chairs opposite the desk. Bernie was a somewhat short, attentive man with a lean face, narrow nose and a slightly mischievous smile like a leprechaun's grin. He was middle-aged and had a slight paunch. Jeffrey was surprised that he was wearing a sweater instead of a coat and tie. Things sure seemed casual around the Institute.

"Well, you did all right on the Rorschach and the hypnotic induction test, but you came out a little defensive on the other ones," said Bernie. "You answered a number of questions on the MMPI to put yourself in an overly-favorable light. For instance this question – 'Every day of the week I read every editorial in my newspaper without ever missing a day.' You answered that one 'yes'. That's one of the so-called 'lie detector' questions."

"But it's true," Jeffrey said in self-defense.

"What's true, you read every single editorial, every day?"

"My father does too, it runs in the family."

"Hmm."

Bernie looked back down at the information on his desk. "Tell me a little about yourself, Jeffrey. Help me get to know you better."

Jeffrey leaned forward and began volunteering all sorts of information – about his past and present grades, which were excellent; his intended major, which was Psychology; his ambition, which was –

"I know all those things already, Jeffrey. What I'd like to hear is something more personal. What about your social life? Do you have a girlfriend?" asked Bernie.

"Well, uhm, no, not at the moment."

"I see. Is there any particular reason for that?"

"No, I just haven't met anyone special since I've been at Princeton," said Jeffrey. "It's not easy to meet girls at an all-male school, if you know what I mean."

"Don't you go to the mixers?"

"Sometimes. They're not the greatest, if you know what I mean."

"Do you always ask people if they know what you mean?"

"What? No. That's just a figure of speech, if you know –" Jeffrey stopped himself.

"Is that something you keep repeating when you get nervous?"

"Uhm, maybe. Sometimes."

"So you don't have a girlfriend at present. What's your opinion of homosexuality?" asked Bernie.

"Uh, I don't know," Jeffrey replied

"Most people have an opinion on that subject."

"Well I guess it's an abnormality. Wouldn't you agree?"

"That depends entirely upon the culture. In ancient Greece, homosexuality was not only considered normal, but admirable. Would you be afraid to admit to natural homosexual tendencies, if you felt them?"

Jam. Crush. Systems overload. "Really, I don't know. Did my tests – ?"

"Your tests were essentially normal."

"Essentially?"

"Except for a tendency toward defensiveness," said Bernie.

"Then I'm not a homosexual?"

"How should I know? Are you?"

"No I'm not."

"You seem to be very sensitive about the subject."

"Not at all. It just doesn't interest me, that's all."

"Part of our research deals with studying how massage therapy impacts the sense of self and body imagery. It's generally referred to as 'Touch Therapy.' Would you have any objection to touching as part of a hypnosis session?"

"I don't know, I never thought about it."

"It's not sexual touching, you understand. By the way, does sex interest you?" Bernie pressed on, digging for information.

"Uhm, sure."

"What else interests you?"

"Well, uhm, monsters."

"Monsters?" said Bernie, his eyebrows shooting upwards.

"Well, monster movies, I mean. My mother would never let me see movies like 'Frankenstein' and 'Dracula,' but movies with monsters were always my favorites – especially movies with giant monsters, like 'King Kong.'"

"Why wouldn't she let you see them?"

"She thought that they would give me nightmares and that I'd become a bed wetter."

"Did you used to wet your bed?"

"Never that I recall. It was just in my mother's mind as a potential problem."

"I see."

"So I started making monster movies of my own. Silent movies with 8mm film. They were about five minutes long, each one. I'd dress up my friends as mummies. We built our own robot out of sheet aluminum. We blew up the Washington Monument with cherry bombs – it was a model we made, of course. I created dragons and dinosaurs – miniatures, but I'd film them to make them look alive. I made about thirty short films starting when I was a kid."

"I see. It sounds rather creative."

"They always said I was creative. And my mother actually likes some of my movies, but not the ones that have blood."

"Blood?" Again, Bernie's eyebrows shot up.

"Well, if one dinosaur tears another one apart, there's lots of blood. We used food coloring. And in our film called 'The Murder Man,' where one of my friends gets stabbed—"

"That's, uh, that's fine," said Bernie. "Fine. And you say you want to be a doctor? Not a film producer?"

"I want to be a psychiatrist, actually. I'm very interested in Sigmund Freud and psychotherapy and all that."

"Well, Jeffrey, I think you'll make a good subject in our research," said Bernie with a little smile.

"Really? That's great."

Bernie cleared his throat. "Tell me, do you have any, uhm, special problems you want to resolve – things about yourself you want to improve?"

"Nothing much. Except maybe – meeting girls."

"I predict you'll find that, once we've worked through some of those defenses of yours, things might start looking up on that score too." He cleared his throat again. He'd been smoking non-stop throughout their meeting. "Now then, the only thing we need before you can begin will be a letter of consent from your parents. All subjects under twenty-one are required to obtain releases from their legal guardians on a form letter."

"Uhm, why is that necessary?"

"Hypnosis is a medical procedure, and every medical procedure carries some risks. That's why we need a release, so we won't have any liability in the event any problem should arise, which is of course highly unlikely. Most of our subjects benefit from hypnosis. Do you foresee any problems getting your parents' permission?"

Problems? No problems that a little forgery couldn't solve, if worst came to worst.

3. Cruising the Loony-Bin

Pok had borrowed the keys to Jonathan's MG, and as usual he'd forgotten to return them. Jonathan had no choice but to scout around the Princeton campus to find him. There was always one most likely place to look, and sure enough, when Jonathan arrived at the basement of the Student Center he found Pok bent over the pool table working on a shot. Good old Pok, World War One leather helmet and goggles in place, aspiring to be the first Zen pool shark.

"Fore!" shouted Jonathan just before Pok hit the ball.

Pok flubbed the shot and turned around scowling, ready to clobber the intruder with the cue stick.

"Sorry, amigo," Jonathan said. "I just couldn't resist."

Seeing who it was, Pok relaxed and took a friendly swing with his cue, missing Jonathan's unflinching head by a calculated three inch margin.

"How about my car keys?" asked Jonathan. "You said you'd drop them by last night."

Pok pulled the goggles up onto his forehead against the leather helmet, reached into his corduroys and tossed Jonathan the keys. "So how about it, up for a few games?"

Jonathan took down a pool stick even though he didn't especially feel like playing – Pok's company always made it worth a round or two. "Just one game, I've got to boogie out to the Institute."

Jonathan broke. The balls scattered. None dropped. Pok eyed the table. "So when are you going to get your brain clear of that loony-bin, hey?"

Jonathan gave him a hard look. "Don't start on that."

Pok pulled the goggles back down over his eyes. He nailed the six-ball with a violent crack of the cue ball. "At least I had enough sense to duck out of that scene. One year as a hypnotic subject was one year too much."

"Bernie retired you because your head was getting strung out from acid, you know that."

"My most honorable accomplishment," Pok replied, lining up another shot and missing.

"If you hadn't weirded out on him, it might be you going out today to get your okay on a draft-deferred job."

"You're crazy, out there getting your brain zapped."

Jonathan looked Pok in the goggled eye, and as usual the tension melted. "With those goggles, you look like one of your Space Brothers gone loony – goes perfect with your moccasins, makes you the first Arapaho astronaut."

Pok grinned his most Pokkian grin. "Your shot, puchito." Jonathan chalked his tip. The two-ball bounced around four corners, knocked in the three-ball and then the ten-ball, and then came to rest right against the eight-ball. Pok grunted his approval. "Not a bad shot for a novice," he said.

Suddenly Pok spun around, as if someone were at the stairs. He went trotting over, Indian on the warpath, and looked up the stairwell. "I heard somebody," he said. "Goddamn Institute's got the CIA on my tail, I know it."

Jonathan went over to check it out. "There's nobody there. Man, are you ever jumpy. You've got to watch it, Pok."

"I can feel it, they're out to pop me."

"I think you should maybe get your dad to put up some money for you to see somebody about the paranoia."

"Hey man, first of all I've got no father. Secondly I've got my own income. Third of all, it's your head that needs help. The Institute is going to leave you a complete zombie."

"I'm not doing any more sessions as a subject. I'm moving up to hypnotist today if Bernie gives me the okay."

"You said you're still having one session a week."

"Don't you even remember the procedure? You went through the deconditioning phase just like I am."

"And that was the worst part of it all."

"How do you know?"

"That's the whole point, Bernie zaps your brain so you don't remember zilch."

Jonathan looked at his watch. "I've got to go," he said, putting his cue stick away. "Catch you later."

Jonathan walked out of the Student Center and into the beautiful autumn morning: thirteenth century England, stone castles passing for lecture halls and dormitories. Wide expanses of green lawns that looked as if they had been designed for Queen Elizabeth's croquet games. Gaping gargoyles leaping from high archways. He shook his longish Beatle-length hair out of his eyes and headed down the path to the parking lot.

There were hardly any students outside – most of them were busy in the lecture halls or deep in the bowels of the library or playing scientist in the chemistry lab or shocking rats over in the Psychology Building. Jonathan looked up at a flock of pigeons winging suddenly overhead toward the steeple of the University Chapel. As his eyes returned to the path, he suddenly felt strange, captivated by all the trees in front of the Art Museum rustling in the breeze, their branches silhouetted against the sky –

The image triggered something in Jonathan's memory. He recalled looking out a window and seeing the infinitely delicate fan-patterns of branches outside, and then looking inside his head and seeing the same patterns in there – his retina or optic nerve or something inside his brain.

He blinked and looked back down at the path, feeling turbulent emotions welling inside him at the sudden flashback. He'd been elated when he first had that direct experience of the inside-outside universe, but now he didn't want it to come back, he just wanted to walk down the path and not have anything happening.

He found the vintage machine that Pok managed to keep running for him through various incantations and occasional open-hood surgery. He warmed up the engine for the prescribed two minutes and then got into driving – buzzing down Nassau Street with his noisy muffler, heading out of the small town and then cruising through sedate hilly farmlands and on into the woods, leaning with the curves, flying along the straight stretches, downshifting at exactly the right rpm, never touching the brakes.

It was almost as good as riding a horse back on the ranch. Sometimes Jonathan thought the MG was definitely an animal in machinery clothing. In fact, it sometimes seemed all the same to him, machine and animal. Bernie had given him a hypnotic condition to be a robot once. He could vaguely remember that now, as he was driving –

Linda gave him a smile as Jonathan walked past the receptionist's desk. "Jonathan, there you are, Bernie's been waiting for you for almost an hour. You were scheduled for eleven."

"Tell Bernie I've got to take a pee. I'll be up in a few." He walked down the corridor of the basement. This was where it had all happened, the six small hypnosis rooms – and this was where he would start working with his own subject soon if Bernie approved him today. The door to the bathroom closed behind him. Silence, except for the sound of the urinal leaking. He flipped on the light. The ventilator fan started up like a helicopter over his head.

He made his way across the room to the john, unzipped, relaxed with a sigh, and commenced firing. Good old phallus. Mainstay of Freudian psychology, mainstay of his summer in San Francisco. Susan in the morning, Susan in the evening, Susan at suppertime.

He suddenly felt a very strange sensation, as though the floor was floating off to one side. Then the walls started pulsing as if they'd come alive and were breathing. Goddamn, he said to himself. Another hallucination – when were they going to stop? All he had to do was walk inside the Institute these days and his sanity took a vacation.

He turned off the light, stood a moment in the stillness of the john, and then went out into the basement hall. He could hear Beatles music playing from a room nearby: 'A Day in the Life.' He listened to the crescendo of the orchestra in the middle of the song ... then the piano with Paul McCartney singing "... found my coat, grabbed my hat, made the bus in seconds flat, found my way upstairs and had a smoke, and somebody spoke and I went into a dream ..."

That's what it'd been like here right from the beginning, Jonathan thought as he let his boots propel him up the stairs ... a hypnotist spoke, and you went into a dream.

"You're an hour late," Bernie said impatiently as Jonathan walked into his office and closed the door behind him.

"I hit a cat on the way out," Jonathan said, making up an excuse that would win sympathy. "Had to stop to bury it."

Bernie gave him an uncertain look, shook his head and dropped his expression of anger. He was wearing his mandala necklace Carl Jung had supposedly given him. He lit a cigarette and inhaled. "So how are you feeling today?" he said. "You sound a little spaced-out."

"I'm just tired. My studies are dragging me down."

"Well then, perhaps we should hold off on considering you as a hypnotist."

"Oh no, that won't be a problem – studying is a drag, I'd rather work out here full-time and just let school drop."

"You can't do that, you need your degree if you plan on continuing out here. Here's my suggestion – you take on your first subject and we'll see how that goes, and once a week we'll spend an afternoon together to go over the deconditioning sessions again. If we repeat the deconditioning, I'm sure you'll be clear."

"Bernie, we agreed – no more conditions."

"I'm not talking about conditions, I'm talking about doing more deconditioning."

"Maybe I don't want to go under at all for a while."

"Jonathan, don't resist me. If you can't take on this job as a hypnotist, you'll be up for the Vietnam draft when you graduate this spring."

"Okay then, whatever it takes."

Bernie inhaled again on his cigarette, which was already getting down to the filter. "So let's do a session."

"Today?"

"Yes, today."

"But –"

"Jonathan, if you're going to resist me –"

"All right – but I promised Coach I'd make it back today for warmups before practice. He's down on my case, we've got a big meet coming up."

"Are you sure you're going to be able to keep up your studies, be a fencer – and also a hypnotist?"

"Sure, no problem."

"Then let's go downstairs. I'll make it a quick one this time. How was your weekend?"

"Okay, the usual."

"Girl?"

"Sorta."

"Well remember, you're not ready for anything serious. Save your energy for this new challenge out here."

Jonathan followed Bernie out of his office and down to the basement, feeling caught. They settled into their familiar roles in the little room, Jonathan in the reclining chair. He knew every nook and cranny of that hypnosis cell, every rust spot on the overhead pipes and every crack on the tiled floor.

Bernie pulled his straight-backed chair over close to Jonathan's side. "Well now, just take a deep breath."

Jonathan felt his resistance melting as sleep already pushed into his body – that seductive peace of the hypnotic trance he'd fallen into so many times that it was now like a second home.

"Take another deep breath ... just listen to my voice, let yourself relax. I'm going to say your hypnotic induction word in a moment, and you'll instantly sink into a deep trance."

Jonathan felt his mind letting go of thoughts, his ears waiting for the word, his breathing getting heavy.

"Callubra-Collorum."

Jonathan felt himself trying to hold on to his awareness, he felt the resistance inside him struggling to hold its ground. But the trance just swept over him, he felt himself drifting deeper and deeper into that familiar womb-like place.

"... more and more peaceful ... calm ... open. A thick white fog is settling over the lake now ... you're at peace ... tired ... giving up all resistance ... listening to my voice as if it were a voice deep inside you ... you're completely asleep, completely under my control ..."

Jonathan was breathing deeply, slowly, sound asleep. Bernie kept talking, using words Jonathan could no longer consciously grasp.

Suddenly there came an explosion of light. Jonathan felt his body blown upwards with the force of a rocket, the pressure squishing him ... then the rocket slowed, the roaring in his ears died down, and a few moments later there was complete quiet, stillness, floating ...

A slight breeze caressed his face. He opened his eyes. He found himself a hundred feet above the Institute building. A swishing sound approached him, a solitary dove flying by. Jonathan felt as if he were floating in a sort of ether, able to feel the wind but not affected by it. His heart was thumping with a mixture of joy and panic. Gravity wasn't pulling him down at all, he was free – more free than the birds.

Muffled words in his ear –

Another explosion of light – release! He soared hundreds of feet higher, to where he could see the small lake on the Institute grounds, the woods beyond, the driveway leading to the outside world – the New Jersey farms – and there was the township of Princeton miles away ... he could see the towers of Princeton University.

More vague words ... and suddenly he was falling, feeling that ultimate nightmare of toppling off a cliff and tumbling downward. He expected to crash into the Institute roof but there was no roof, no crash, just a soft settling sensation – a sense of returning as he felt the solidity of his body on the chair.

"You are now in your body again ... focus your attention on your breathing in ... out ... in ... good. Feel your heart beating. Your eyelids are becoming less heavy, you're emerging from a beautiful dream – and now you're waking up. As usual we'll talk about your experiences, and then I will hypnotize you again for the memory erasure condition. You're starting to open your eyes, your eyes are opening now ... good – there, how do you feel?"

Jonathan looked around him. He looked up at Bernie who was smiling down at him, beaming with eagerness. Bernie's face at first looked distorted, like a grimacing devil with bulging eyes and puffy lips. "Uhm," Jonathan said, knowing he was supposed to respond.

"Tell me what happened."

From upstairs, the faint sound of the Beatles: "I'm fixing a hole where the rain gets in and stops my mind from wandering, where it will go ..."

Jonathan cleared his throat. Bernie certainly didn't look menacing anymore. He seemed to have an expression of genuine interest. "Uhm, well – it was amazing, I really did it, I left my body, I was up there looking down at you, at us. I mean, I was blown completely up out of the building, I was up there, Bernie, I was up there, I really was!"

"Very good. Okay, you can close your eyes, and when I say your word, you will go immediately back into a deep trance for the memory erasure ... good, eyes closed, yes – Callubra-Callorum ..." There was a long moment of silence. Then Bernie's voice continued. "You are now in a very deep trance. I am going to remove all memories of this experience from your conscious mind. You will have no recall that you experienced an out-of-body condition or anything else that we've done in this session, unless I specifically ask you to remember it later on. So now the fog is again growing thicker ... whiter ... coming over you ... engulfing your mind and erasing your memory of the experience you had under this condition ... there's just the great white fog which only I can remove ..."

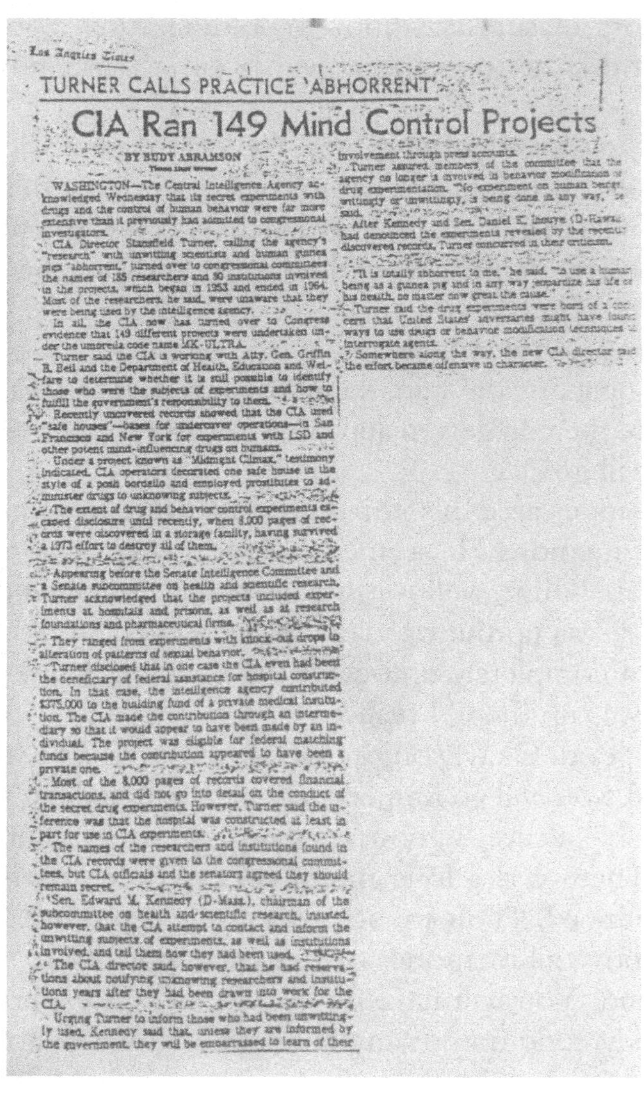

Los Angeles Times

TURNER CALLS PRACTICE 'ABHORRENT'

CIA Ran 149 Mind Control Projects

BY BUDY ABRAMSON

WASHINGTON—The Central Intelligence Agency acknowledged Wednesday that its secret experiments with drugs and the control of human behavior were far more extensive than it previously had admitted to congressional investigators.

CIA Director Stansfield Turner, calling the agency's "research" with unwitting scientists and human guinea pigs "abhorrent," turned over to congressional committees the names of 185 researchers and 80 institutions involved in the projects, which began in 1953 and ended in 1964. Most of the researchers, he said, were unaware that they were being used by the intelligence agency.

In all, the CIA now has turned over to Congress evidence that 149 different projects were undertaken under the umbrella code name MK-ULTRA.

Turner said the CIA is working with Atty. Gen. Griffin B. Bell and the Department of Health, Education and Welfare to determine whether it is still possible to identify those who were the subjects of experiments and how to fulfill the government's responsibility to them.

Recently uncovered records showed that the CIA used "safe houses"—bases for undercover operations—in San Francisco and New York for experiments with LSD and other potent mind-influencing drugs on humans.

Under a project known as "Midnight Climax," testimony indicated, CIA operators decorated one safe house in the style of a posh bordello and employed prostitutes to administer drugs to unknowing subjects.

The extent of drug and behavior control experiments escaped disclosure until recently, when 8,000 pages of records were discovered in a storage facility, having survived a 1973 effort to destroy all of them.

Appearing before the Senate Intelligence Committee and a Senate subcommittee on health and scientific research, Turner acknowledged that the projects included experiments at hospitals and prisons, as well as at research foundations and pharmaceutical firms.

They ranged from experiments with knock-out drops to alteration of patterns of sexual behavior.

Turner disclosed that in one case the CIA even had been the beneficiary of federal assistance for hospital construction. In that case, the intelligence agency contributed $375,000 to the building fund of a private medical institution. The CIA made the contribution through an intermediary so that it would appear to have been made by an individual. The project was eligible for federal matching funds because the contribution appeared to have been a private one.

Most of the 8,000 pages of records covered financial transactions, and did not go into detail on the conduct of the secret drug experiments. However, Turner said the inference was that the hospital was constructed at least in part for use in CIA experiments.

The names of the researchers and institutions found in the CIA records were given to the congressional committees, but CIA officials and the senators agreed they should remain secret.

Sen. Edward M. Kennedy (D-Mass.), chairman of the subcommittee on health and scientific research, insisted, however, that the CIA attempt to contact and inform the unwitting subjects of experiments, as well as institutions involved, and tell them how they had been used.

The CIA director said, however, that he had reservations about notifying unknowing researchers and institutions years after they had been drawn into work for the CIA.

Urging Turner to inform those who had been unwittingly used, Kennedy said that, unless they are informed by the government, they will be embarrassed to learn of their involvement through press accounts.

Turner assured members of the committee that the agency no longer is involved in behavior modification or drug experimentation. "No experiment on human beings, wittingly or unwittingly, is being done in any way," he said.

After Kennedy and Sen. Daniel K. Inouye (D-Hawaii) had denounced the experiments revealed by the recently discovered records, Turner concurred in their criticism.

"It is totally abhorrent to me," he said, "to use a human being as a guinea pig and in any way jeopardize his life or his health, no matter how great the cause."

Turner said the drug experiments were born of a concern that United States' adversaries might have found ways to use drugs or behavior modification techniques to interrogate agents.

Somewhere along the way, the new CIA director said, the effort became offensive in character.

Los Angeles Times Thurs., July 21, 1977 —Part I 21

WANTED TO SILENCE EX-AGENTS

CIA Once Sought Amnesia Drug

BY NORMAN KEMPSTER
Times Staff Writer

WASHINGTON—As part of an 11-year program of experiments in techniques of mind control, the CIA attempted in the early 1950s to develop a drug that would make former employes forget the agency's secrets, CIA documents disclosed Wednesday.

The papers, made public because of a request under the Freedom of Information Act, showed that the program—codenamed MK ULTRA—had been far more extensive than the drug tests disclosed two years ago by the Rockefeller Commission.

In addition to studying drugs ranging from amnesia drops to aphrodisiacs, the CIA sought to develop techniques for behavior modification through radiation, electric shock and "harassment substances."

A major goal of the program, begun in 1953 and ended in 1964, was to develop a combination of drugs and hypnotism that would break down prisoners' resistance to interrogation. The papers indicated that those techniques had been used to question at least two Russian agents and probably other persons.

The minutes of a secret meeting of CIA officials on July 15, 1953, included discussion of techniques for making a person forget what he knew so he could not disclose it intentionally or inadvertantly.

"(Name deleted) states that some individuals in the agency had to know tremendous amounts of information and if any way could be found to produce amnesia for this type of information—for instance, after the individual had left the agency—it would be a remarkable thing," the minutes said.

"(Name deleted) and (name deleted) both explained that work was continually being done in an effort to produce controlled amnesias by various means," the report added.

There is no evidence the experiments ever produced a reliable amnesia drug.

The documents were culled from about 1,000 pages of papers released to John Marks, a former State Department intelligence officer and coauthor of "The CIA and the Cult of Intelligence," under the Freedom of Information Act.

The CIA told Marks June 24 that it had found 5,000 additional pages of papers concerning MK ULTRA and a companion program, MK DELTA, which would be released by the end of this month.

Marks said he was certain that the 5,000 pages were the additional documents that CIA Director Stansfield Turner had said last week had been discovered by a "diligent employe" searching through the agency's "retired archives."

The first official word of CIA experimentation with drugs was issued in 1975, when a commission headed by then-Vice President Nelson A. Rockefeller reported that the agency had given LSD to persons who were unaware they were receiving drugs. The report said one person, later identified as an Army scientist named Frank Olson, had committed suicide after drinking an after-dinner liqueur laced with LSD.

The Senate Intelligence Committee headed by Sen. Frank Church (D-Ida.) later described the program in greater detail.

The latest batch of documents, however, includes a 1963 report by then-CIA Inspector General J.S. Earman that said the program, then 10 years old, had investigated "many additional avenues to the control of human behavior . . . including radiation, electroshock, various fields of psychology, psychiatry, sociology, and anthropology, graphology, harassment substances and paramilitary devices and materials."

The same report listed some results of the program: "As of 1960, no effective knockout pill was known to exist, (but) truth serum, aphrodisiac or recruitment pill was known to exist."

Although MK ULTRA officially began in 1953, the documents contained several reports showing an earlier CIA interest in drugs and related matters.

In a letter addressed "Dear Bill," a CIA operative whose name was deleted described on Nov. 29, 1949, a series of ways of committing murder and getting away with it.

"I believe that there are two chemical substances which would be most useful in that they would leave no characteristic pathologic findings and the quantities needed could be easily transported to places where they were to be used," the letter said.

"One of these, sodium fluoroacetate when ingested in sufficient quantities to cause death, does not cause characteristic pathologic lesions . . . The other chemical substance which I have in mind is tetraethyl lead, which, as you know, could be dropped on the skin in very small quantities, producing no local lesion, and after a quick death no specific pathologic evidence . . . would be present."

The operative then turned to more exotic methods. He said that if an individual could be put into a tightly sealed room with a block of dry ice, "It is highly probable that his death would result and that there would be no chances of circumstances being detected." And there were more primitive methods: "Smother the victim with a pillow or strangle him with a wide piece of cloth, such as a bath towel."

Several of the documents indicated that the CIA had entered the field of behavior modification in an effort to match programs of the Soviet Union. One purpose of the drug tests was to find ways of defending U.S. agents against possible use of drugs or other techniques by the Russians.

On July 14, 1952, a CIA memo described the interrogation, using a combination of drugs and hypnosis, of "two experienced, professional-type agents suspected of working for Soviet intelligence." In both cases, the memo said, the agents disclosed their activities, some dating back 15 years.

Earlier reports on the CIA program said drugs had been given to narcotics addicts, alcoholics, prison inmates and others, often without their knowledge. The new documents describe one series of tests in a prison.

The Senate Intelligence Committee, headed by Sen. Daniel K. Inouye (D-Hawaii), is to conduct a hearing on the MK ULTRA documents July 28. But a spokesman said the session might be moved up, perhaps to as early as next Monday.

Albert Einstein accepted a faculty position at Princeton's Institute for Advanced Study in 1932, and he lived on Mercer Street in Princeton until his death in 1955. His hairstyle was far ahead of its time and was more appropriate to the 'Psychedelic Era' of the mid-to-late 1960's that would follow him.

4. Civilizations Come, Civilizations Go

When Jeffrey arrived for his first hypnosis session, Mike told him that he was going to be trained by a fellow Princeton undergraduate, a senior named John Selby but everyone called him Jonathan for reasons still unknown. "He's a Psych major, fencing team star, grew up on a cattle ranch out west," Mike told Jeffrey with just a touch of condescension. "Rides horses."

"Sounds interesting."

"You could call him that. He completed his full year as a hypnotic subject, he was one of Bernie's top performers – great data! And now we've put him through rigorous training as a research hypnotist, Dr. Osmond himself worked with him for several weeks – so the 'psychedelic cowboy' will do you good, I assure you. That's Bernie's nickname for Jonathan. Do come to me if you have any questions – agreed?"

"Oh, well – of course."

"So go wait in the library like last time."

The library was silent. The librarian, an older short stout woman, eyed him but avoided conversation. While looking vaguely through a hypnosis book, Jeffery saw an elderly thin white-haired man flutter in like a big bird, quickly take some books from a shelf and then disappear out the door in the twinkling of an eye without making a single peep.

"Oh, who was that?" Jeffrey asked the librarian.

"That was Dr. Osmond. Humphry we call him. He's in charge of all this, over Bernie and everyone."

"I read about him," Jeffry confessed. "He's quite a controversial, unorthodox psychiatric theorist. I read that he knew Aldous Huxley, the philosopher."

"Quite right, good friends to the end."

"Mike told me not to read anything by Dr. Osmond – or any other psychiatrist or psychologist on the Institute staff. Or I might unconsciously prejudice the research results."

There was Linda in the doorway. "We found Jonathan," she told him abruptly. "He was here the whole time, upstairs on the roof. Just go down to the end of the second floor hall past Bernie's office and climb out the window," she instructed.

Making only two wrong turns, Jeffrey located the window and climbed out. It was a nice place to sit in the sun, with an unobstructed view of the lake and woods. And there, sitting cross-legged on a cushion with his eyes closed, was the person Jeffrey assumed was Jonathan. He had longish hair but not real long. Sort of Beatle length, pre-'Sgt. Pepper.' He was good-looking with his shirt off, probably had no trouble at all making passes at neat chicks, thought Jeffrey.

Jonathan's eyes suddenly popped open.

"Hi," said Jeffrey, smiling. "Are you Jonathan?"

"Most of the time," came the cryptic reply. "You must be my subject."

"Paul Jeffrey, first and middle name, but everyone calls me Jeffrey."

"How come?"

"Hard to remember. I think it's because I always felt Paul was too Biblical – you know, Saint Paul of the New Testament – and Davids reminds everybody of King David of the Israelites. I'm ethnically Jewish but I'm not into religion at all – so somewhere along the line I asked people to call me Jeffrey. "

"Okay, it's Jeffrey then. Have a seat."

Jeffrey sat on a cushion across from him.

"Hey, look over there!" Jonathan said, pointing across the lake. "There's a doe running behind those willow trees. We're far enough out in the country here, there are a few deer left." He stared off into space a moment, then turned his head back to Jeffrey. "So how are you doing at the old monastery?"

"You mean Princeton? Okay, I guess."

"Been hitting the mixers?"

"On and off. Mostly off."

"Those mixers really show the sickness of this society – but what the hell – civilizations come, civilizations go. So what's your passion when you're not studying or going to mixers or getting involved in subvertive research?"

"Subvertive?" said Jeffrey.

"Not a word? Should be."

"Well, I've made movies ever since I was about ten."

"Really? What kind of movies?"

"Monster movies, mainly. I love special effects. You know, dragons and dinosaurs. Frankenstein and Dracula. They're just eight millimeter and they don't have sound of course. But my friends and I have made dozens of them. I even won an amateur film contest from a national magazine."

"Good going. For me, I don't go out of my way to get scared – life's scary enough as it is. I prefer the Zen mode, trying to stay balanced, working at getting at least somewhat self-aware."

"Working like you do at this Institute must be a perfect place to become self-aware. Mike told me that even Timothy Leary comes out here sometimes to do LSD or hypnosis sessions with Dr. Osmond. I read about Timothy Leary in Time Magazine."

"Well yeah, lots of people come through here, Humphry is the epicenter of psychedelic research – and Timothy Leary definitely needs help keeping his trip together. He's a bit pushy if you ask me, telling everybody that acid's no big thing when in reality it can scare you shitless, at least it did that to me once."

"I'd definitely be scared to try something like that. And my mother would go into mourning if she found out."

"You do understand that you're not supposed to take acid while you're a subject here. At least, not officially."

"Yes, Mike told me."

"Of course off the record, Humphry does still guide people now and then, and he helped me a lot with guided LSD trips. Really a lot. He even guided Aldous Huxley. And he's friends with Alan Watts, an amazing philosopher who I've talked with three times when he came in from the West Coast. We even got stoned at a party Bernie threw for Alan last month. Alan is from England originally, and he studied Zen in New York."

"*Like Zen and the Art of Motorcycle Maintenance*?"

"Yep. Have you read it?"

"I did. Fascinating."

"Zen is the most sensible world view I've ever encountered. It puts you right into the eternal now, wipes away all other thoughts. Total awareness. Anyway, believe it or not, Alan Watts was once an Episcopal priest, and then he left the ministry. He teaches at the American Academy of Asian Studies. He really inspired me to adopt Zen as my approach to fencing – I'm on the Princeton fencing team – but my coach thinks Zen fencing is crazy, doesn't understand it at all. You know, in a way, Alan Watts feels to me like the father I wish my dad was – but between you and me, right now things have gotten tense around here. Alan came here unexpectedly last week, and he and Humphry had some kind of argument – but let's not get into that."

"And what about Bernie? What does he think of Alan Watts and Zen and all that?"

"Oh Bernie's another issue altogether."

"What do you mean?"

"Oh – nothing. If we start talking about Bernie, we'll be up on this roof until next week. What do you say, let's go downstairs and get to work."

They went inside and down a flight of stairs and then down more stairs. "How did you happen to end up on the East Coast going to Princeton?" Jeffrey asked as they descended side by side.

"I'd read the University had a polo team. My mom had always loved polo, she grew up at a fancy horse place in Connecticut. Foxen Place. But when I got here I found out the Administration had given the polo team the axe. Things never turn out the way they're advertised."

Jonathan led them into one of six small rooms in the basement. He didn't turn on the light but there was a window high up providing illumination. "We'll have to do something about this cell," Jonathan said, as he closed the door.

It certainly was barren, thought Jeffrey, noticing the plumbing exposed against the ceiling and undecorated walls. At least there was a carpet on the floor, and the reclining chair looked comfortable.

"I've got a poster of the Beatles I could bring," Jeffrey offered. "It's them standing on the sidewalk in front of Buckingham Palace. I've got their new album – 'Sergeant Pepper's Lonely Hearts Club Band.' It's fantastic."

"The Beatles are influencing more people than President Johnson or the Pope or anybody. Sit down there, make yourself at home. I'm into George Harrison," Jonathan volunteered. "Pok is helping me learn some of George's bottleneck licks. I totally dig slide."

"Me too, and he's my favorite Beatle."

Jonathan pulled down the window shade, struck a wooden match and lit a candle. "So – you want to get hypnotized."

"Yeah, I hope I'm good at it."

"Don't worry, that's my job."

"Dr. Aaronson told me that you were a subject here last year. Who was your hypnotist?"

"Bernie. Dr. Aaronson – everyone calls him Bernie. He'll probably work with you too, once you're fully trained. Learning to get into a trance is just the preliminary part. It's the conditions that are heavy. The ones with Bernie will blow you away. They did me anyway."

"Mike said you'll erase my memory of what happens, I won't remember what the conditions were afterwards."

"While you're in training I'll let you remember a few. I'm not gung-ho on the memory-erasing thing."

"There's nothing wrong with it, is there? You've got to do it for the research design, right?"

"That's the party line. You smoke cigarettes?"

"Never."

"Good, I can't handle cigarette smoke. Worse than the smog in L.A." Jonathan lit a match and then touched it to a stick of incense. "You ever been in L.A.?"

"Not yet. I've never been west of Cincinnati. I spent a summer there studying clarinet at the Cincinnati Conservatory of Music. They've got some pretty incredible Gaiety Theaters there."

"What's a Gaiety Theater?"

"A strip show. And you can get in when you're only sixteen, which I was at the time. The guys and I would go every week. But the girls used pasties. On their nipples."

"Every week, a strip show? With pasties? Sounds like a poor substitute for having a girlfriend."

"Yeah, but sometimes you have to take what you can get, if you know what I mean. As for Los Angeles, I really hope to get there some day. To see Hollywood, you know."

"L.A. is totally out of its gourd. People running around hyped on smog and not even aware that their consciousness is being altered by it, like taking uppers and downers at the same time and thinking you're straight. Know what I mean?"

"I think so."

"What's your dad do anyway?" asked Jonathan.

"He's a professor of diplomatic history at Georgetown University. He'd like me to become a scholar too but I'm more interested in being a psychiatrist."

"That means four years of med school. The Buddha attained enlightenment in less time than that. Are you aware of your left foot right now?"

Jeffrey was startled at the question -- the sudden change of the topic of conversation, hitting him like whiplash.

"My left foot? Uh, yes."

"Before I asked you?"

"Uh, no."

"So okay, take a deep breath, and now slowly exhale ... good ... inhale ... allow your awareness to expand – start at your head, and now slowly allow your awareness to move down your spine. Just relax and let your thoughts become more and more quiet ... feel the energy, the life force pulsing all through your body, all the way down, down to the tips of your toes. You don't have to do anything at all, you're completely safe, relaxed, calm – focus your attention on your left foot. Tighten your foot. Feel that energy, that tension. And now relax it. Tighten ... relax. Now your other foot. Tighten ... relax ..."

Jonathan worked on setting up the Princeton University Student Committee on Mental Health, which published this pamphlet on psychedelic drug use on campus. It came to the attention of a New York Times editor and even made the CBS evening news, resulting in an invitation for Jonathan to speak with Princeton University President Robert F. Goheen about psychedelic drugs. Robert Goheen went on to become President Nixon's Ambassador to India a few years later.

5. Dusting the Diencephalon

Nassau Hall is one of the places they show everyone on the guided tour of Princeton. Visitors learn that during the Revolutionary War it served as military headquarters for George Washington for a time, and later it became the temporary Capitol of the United States. Outside the main entrance, two stone tigers stand poised for attack, guarding the historic building from undesirable spirits.

Jonathan walked up the ancient stone steps, worn down about two inches from being trod upon by so many famous patriots. He had been summoned to Nassau Hall for a private meeting with the President of the University, Robert F. Goheen, concerning a questionnaire survey of Princeton students using marijuana and psychedelic drugs that Jonathan had conducted. It had been funded by the National Institutes of Health, which, as far as Jonathan was aware at that time, also funded Dr. Osmond's research. Jonathan had analyzed the data and discovered a number of facts that had shocked the Board of Trustees of the university. Using the Psychology Department's computer to cross-check his statistics, he'd proved that students who had adopted the 'psychedelic lifestyle' as defined in his research paper had higher grade averages than 'straight' students and a number were on the Dean's List.

He'd agreed at first to keep his findings confidential, the University definitely wanted to hush up his discovery, which disproved the media and government myth that marijuana and psychedelic use ruined one's chances of success in life – in fact they seemed to do the opposite, at least at Princeton, and Jonathan felt that the world had a right to know. He'd been brought up to be honest and not to hide the truth, so in typical impulsive Jonathan mode, he'd shared his research with a college friend whose dad worked at the New York Times, and they'd immediately done a front-page article on the use of marijuana and LSD at Princeton.

Jonathan had been quoted several times in the article, expounding on Humphry Osmond's theories about altered states of consciousness. That publicity had gotten him in very hot water out at the Institute – Bernie almost fired him on the spot. And now President Goheen had called him in for a one-on-one talk. Jonathan went through the imposing oak doors of Nassau Hall, stomped across the spacious lobby in his worn boots and paused in front of the receptionist. "I'm here to see President Goheen," he said.

In a few moments, he was ushered down the main corridor to the door labeled THE PRESIDENT. The bespectacled, rather slight pillar of Princeton University was behind his desk awaiting Jonathan's arrival – the man's father and grandfather had both been Presbyterian ministers, and he looked of similar sober stock. He stood up, came around his desk to Jonathan and shook his hand.

"Good to see you again, Jonathan," he said in a friendly but formal tone of voice.

Jonathan wondered where President Goheen had seen him before – he'd of course seen the president giving speeches, playing Rah-Rah-Charlie at basketball games, out there cheering for basketball star Bill Bradley to dunk another one for Princeton and all that. But he was certain that they had never formally met. Maybe he'd come to the fencing championships last year.

"Thanks for inviting me," Jonathan responded, feeling more nervous than he'd expected.

"Won't you have a seat?"

The office had fine paneling and plush chairs, well-lit pictures of former presidents of the university, one red rose in a crystal vase and a mammoth uncluttered walnut desk.

"How are your studies coming along this year, Jonathan?"

"Okay, I suppose. Nothing to get excited about."

"You're in Psychology, I understand."

"Right."

"Well, I appreciate your finding time to have a chat with me about drug use on campus. I want you to understand that except for that study I okayed last semester, I'm still mostly ignorant of the subject. And I was naturally quite alarmed to see the piece in the New York Times. A boy was treated in the infirmary just last month who'd had a 'bad trip' I think you call it. Apparently he was hysterical for almost an hour until a sedative calmed him down. Dr. Dalrymple said you know the fellow."

"You must be talking about Pok."

"I hope he's recovering satisfactorily."

"He's fine. Somebody freaked him, that's all. Problem is, the doctors in the infirmary don't know how to handle an LSD freakout."

"Dr. Dalrymple was telling me only yesterday that the infirmary is researching how to handle this new problem."

"You need someone who really knows how to talk people down when they freak out, it's a simple hypnotic process. I work out at a research center under Dr. Humphry Osmond who's an expert on all of that."

"Yes, I spoke with him earlier today on the phone. Perhaps we can discuss that possibility, I understand you have professional experience related to all this. I've asked you here today because I quite honestly need your help in gaining deeper insight into our small student minority involved with drugs."

"A lot of students use speed to cram for exams, and of course alcohol all the time. And a bit of pot like my study showed. I mostly don't use drugs in general, just now and then the psychoactive insight-inducing ones, LSD and mescaline. They're quite special – and they need to be approached correctly to ensure a positive experience – proper set and setting. That's been clarified by Dr. Osmond, he says a good set and setting are essential – otherwise you can easily have a freakout like Pok did."

"Oh. I see. Tell me more," President Goheen asked, steadily digging for information. "What does all this mean to you personally?"

"Well my major interest is formal psychedelic research," Jonathan told him honestly. "EEG studies of the effects of LSD, hypnotic induction of altered states of consciousness, things like that."

"And how can I best educate myself in all this?"

"That depends on how deep you want to go."

President Goheen leaned forward in his chair and folded his hands over his knees. "Foremost on my mind is determining the extent that use of these drugs constitutes a health hazard to students on campus. I need to find out why my students are interested in using drugs at all – is there some campus situation that's driving them to drugs, some new difficulty that's my responsibility to correct? Obviously the problem is a complex one, I don't expect simple answers."

"I'd definitely recommend that, for medical and psychological data, you rely on Dr. Osmond, or Dr. Aaronson. Or Carl Pfeiffer, he's Deputy Director of the Institute's Bureau of Research. He did a ten-year study, since 1955, giving LSD to prisoners at the Bordentown Reformatory and a penitentiary in Atlanta."

"Is that a fact?"

"I know him, I could arrange a meeting."

"That's a good suggestion – let's do it. Now regarding the question of why Princeton students are interested in these so-called 'psychedelic' drugs – could you give me some personal insight into that?"

"On my part, I guess I took psychedelics because I wanted to experience expanded spiritual states of consciousness that my cultural upbringing repressed. Mystical experiences, things like that. In my freshman year, just before Christmas, a professor from Harvard, Richard Alpert from the psych department up there, came down and gave a talk to a small group of students about stimulating deep spiritual experience. What LSD does is, it temporarily loosens all the inhibitions that keep us from directly experiencing who we really are beyond our cultural blinders."

"Blinders? Perhaps those inhibitions serve a function, they help make us rational human beings rather than un-thinking wild animals."

"Columbus didn't discover America by getting freaked-out about the size of the Atlantic Ocean. I came to college here because I want some real direct experience of who I am, not just textbook ramblings. No offense."

Jonathan's answer made President Goheen sit back in his chair. "I just can't understand, Jonathan," he said, shaking his head. "Where are we failing you? What academic needs aren't we meeting?"

"It's not a matter of academic needs," Jonathan said emphatically. "It's a matter of altered states of consciousness."

"And just what exactly do you mean by that?"

Jonathan remembered how Dr. Osmond had explained it to him, back when he was so wet behind the ears he didn't even know what a 'trip' was. "So like, all your life you've seen things one way, experienced life in one pattern, bought into one set of beliefs – and thought that what you perceived was reality, right?

But if you take LSD or something similar that temporarily expands your consciousness, you can really see what's real. New research up at Harvard is showing that while on acid, all culturally-programmed filters in the diencephalon temporarily dissolve into a vast infinity of realities. Take perception – you see everything here now as stable, right, not moving or flowing?"

"Well, yes, that's the way it is."

"But no – your eyes, your optic nerves, your brain, all work together to create the illusion that you call reality. I know Ralph Abramson in the physics department, he describes scientific reality just that same way. Psychedelics help us understand that what we normally experience is actually just a tiny bit of reality, a vague illusion. The diencephalon – that part of the brain which controls incoming sensations and memories – usually decides automatically what you'll experience and what you won't. The amygdala is a very primitive part of the brain, it only lets into your consciousness the particular perceptions and thoughts that have traditional survival value. All creativity, for instance, is based on getting the diencephalon to temporarily relax its hold on your mind. Once you manage to expand your consciousness by whatever means, you come to realize that there's so much more to life than what the diencephalon has been letting you experience."

The President peered at Jonathan over his bifocals. "Well, you sound erudite on the topic – but I simply cannot grasp why you feel this compulsion to escape from reality. I myself have always treasured our spiritual heritage and American traditions, I've never had any desire to distort my God-given perceptions of the world. You're saying that my entire life is a product of some part of my brain that doesn't let me see things the way they are. I simply cannot agree with you. This whole so-called psychedelic movement sounds like a last-ditch attempt to escape from the real pressures of life – pressures we all have to deal with in order to survive. What would happen to our country if everyone started 'expanding his consciousness,' as you put it, and no one was left to maintain the basic structure of our culture?"

"I'm not really all that interested in maintaining the old order of this culture," said Jonathan. "Sorry – that sounds harsh. But look at what the old order always brings us – war, inequality, people fighting each other, grabbing what they can for themselves. Maybe the psychedelics can help us evolve beyond all that – either that or it's all over anyway."

President Goheen leaned back in his chair and took a deep breath. "Well, that was a mouthful, Jonathan. But all that aside, at the very basic level of scholastic decency and proper protocol, you must know that releasing that article to the New York Times last week seriously damaged the reputation of Princeton University."

"I thought that the truth should out, regardless of the consequences. Isn't that a basic precept of the University?"

"Oh Jonathan. You try to offer sharp answers – but deep down I still see a young man running away from reality rather than facing it. I know there are many problematic aspects of our era which are disturbing to sensitive, intelligent young men of your generation, the war in Vietnam especially. But we must stand up for our values and traditions, not denigrate them. I only hope that you'll realize, before it's too late for your own career in psychology, that escapism has never been and it never will be a constructive solution to any real problem."

"Yeah, well. Sorry. I guess we just see things very differently."

The conversation fell into a painful silence.

"So then, anyway, I thank you for coming by," President Goheen said tersely, obviously not pleased with the outcome of the discourse. "Perhaps we can talk later, once I've met with

Dr. Osmond or Dr. Pfeiffer. In the meantime, please, do not publicize any information you gather here or at the Institute without my permission. Do you understand? I do care about you, I'm here for you. Please come talk any time. Dr. Dalrymple at the Infirmary says the same. When you need help, it's important to have the courage to ask."

He got up, gave Jonathan a gung-ho Princeton handshake and a paternal pat on the back, and he escorted him out of his office. "Good luck," he said.

The President's secretary gave Jonathan a strange look as he walked past her desk. Jonathan gave her a strange look back.

Outside the air was cool and ready for gasping, and Jonathan did so – feeling shaky after the confrontation, somehow hurt that President Goheen had been so deaf to what he'd tried to explain. His own dad was even worse. At least Jonathan had survived in the heat of the lion's den. And the President had come across as at least striving to be somewhat fair and open-minded. He was just stuck with faulty cultural programming and pre-scientific data to work with, at least as far as Jonathan saw the situation.

And so it was that Jonathan was lost in thought when he approached his old MG in the lower student parking lot. He vaguely noticed two middle-aged short-haired be-suited men leaning against his vehicle, but he didn't actively process the information until it was too late – until he was face to face with them.

"There you are Jonathan," the short fat one said to him in a high but resonant voice, maybe a Boston accent, purposefully standing between Jonathan and the door of the MG. He was right in Jonathan's face from the get-go.

"Uhm, who are you guys? If you'll excuse me, that's my car and —"

"Ease up. We've been assigned to keep a close eye on your recent activities."

"Assigned? Which activities are you talking about?"

"To focus on one area in particular, let's start with drugs. You do take drugs, don't you?"

"So – you're FBI?" No response. "State cops?" said Jonathan, his heart starting to pound. He felt himself starting to lose his cool, so he took a deep breath and calmed himself as best he could under the circumstances.

"Wrong both times," said Shorty.

"Well please – just move aside, I have to get to work."

"We know all about your work," the short one continued.

"Nice to formally meet you, by the way," said the tall thin one in a very sarcastic tone. "We're what you might call your guardian angels."

"Guardian angels?" said Jonathan. "What the hell is that supposed to mean?"

"We've been watching you for some time."

"Did you have a good talk with the Big Man in that nice office in Nassau Hall?" asked Shorty.

"Wait a minute. Wait just a goddamn minute," said Jonathan. "Are you implying that President Goheen picked up the phone to call you after my meeting with him, and –"

"Wrong again," Shorty informed him. "What are you majoring in here, cowboy? Jumping to conclusions? The fact is that you were trusted with research of a highly confidential nature, and yet, in violation of your own Institute rules and university agreement, you chose last week to divulge very sensitive information to the New York Times –"

The taller one piped up all of a sudden, cutting off his colleague in order to finish the sentence. "—thereby endangering the very people we do in fact work with."

"Fuck – you're CIA. Pok was right."

"CIA, that's a good one!" said the tall one to Shorty.

"By the way, your friend Pok – tell him for us," said the short one, "that he is going to be so right someday that maybe he's going to have to vanish."

"What – you're threatening him?"

"I'm standing here telling you," the short one said right back at him, obviously the major-league talker of the two, "that quite apart from our past problems and future concerns with Pok, we are quite displeased with you in particular."

"So now you are threatening me – and I'm going to get the proctors. They'll find out who you are."

At this, the tall one walked right up to Jonathan. "You are not hearing my colleague quite clearly," he said in a very quiet, even monotone voice that Jonathan found much more intimidating than Shorty. "We are simply telling you to cease and desist in certain areas and all shall go well with you. At least for now. Who knows, you might even get that magic draft deferment you're fishing so hard for, you yellow chicken-shit psychedelic cowboy. Yeah, we know psychedelic cowboy is your nickname out at the Institute. We know everything. Do you understand me? And now hear this – if you step out of line just one more time –"

He clapped his hands together so loudly it sounded like a gunshot. The short, fat one threw Jonathan a glare and then turned and started walking away, his tall buddy tailing right after him.

Jonathan gulped for fresh air, got into his aging sports car, cranked it into action and took off like a cowboy bat heading out of Ivy League hell.

6. Jeffrey's Quick

Jeffrey was busy writing in the hypnosis training-session diary that Jonathan had asked him to keep:

Jonathan is letting me remember a lot that happens in these early training sessions. They're so amazing! And he's trying to establish a trance-induction word - a word that I won't remember that will trigger my dropping down into a very deep trance almost instantly. The first couple times, I remembered it, so he keeps changing the word and trying again. Jonathan said Bernie programmed him with a trance-induction word last year, and that it still works for him.

When I sit down in the chair, I now know to let all my emotions drain away. I can be nervous or jumpy when I'm driving out to the Institute, but as soon as I sit down in the hypnosis chair now, all other thoughts go away. Jonathan uses a technique of counting, to take me to deeper and deeper trance states. He'll count from one to ten to reach a certain level. Then he'll go through the letters of the alphabet, with each letter being a more and more relaxed state of deep peace. I just concentrate on his voice and experience whatever he suggests to me. I've come to trust him completely. His voice is my guide.

He gave me another trance-induction word in the session today, and this time I couldn't remember it when he woke me up. He told me the word would be covered by a great white fog – a fog so thick I couldn't see through it. It worked. I tried to remember the word, thinking hard, but it wouldn't come to mind.

Jeffrey closed his hypnosis notebook as Jonathan and Mike entered the hypnosis cell carrying cups of coffee. This would be his sixth session. Mike Kerner had been an observer the last two sessions. Jonathan had turned Jeffrey over to Mike on one occasion to be hypnotized, so Mike could evaluate Jeffrey's progress.

"Today I'm going to take you into some new realms, with Jonathan observing," said Mike. "Do you know what age regression is?"

"Something to do with early memories?"

"It's the experience of reliving an earlier part of your life so vividly you feel as though it's happening all over again. Today we're going to explore things that happened when you were very young. Ready?"

"Sure."

"So just relax, and when I say your trance induction word, you'll go into a deep trance, just as if Jonathan were saying it. Just watch your breathing, let your eyes close ... you're floating quietly, safely along a peaceful stream ... you're completely relaxed ... Kambastena-mondora..."

Jeffrey felt his breaths coming and going and at the same time felt the two nonsense words relaxing him as he floated down a river, without any worries at all, just rocking gently in the current, drifting happily. Mike's voice was distant, soft and almost angelic.

"You are going back ... floating off into your childhood, back to when you were four years old."

Jeffrey floated for a few more breaths without anything happening at all – and then he rose upwards and found himself in nursery school, rushing to get to the toy chest that was filled with wooden milk bottles.

"What's happening, Jeffrey?" Mike's voice quietly asked.

"Uhm. I'm in nursery school. We're playing. It's my turn."

"What are you playing?"

"Milk bottles. I'm the milkman."

"Can you see your teacher?"

"Yes."

"What's her name?"

"Mrs. McCaferty," said Jeffrey. "She's talking to a lady. I want to ask her if it's okay for me to be the milkman."

"Go ahead."

Silence.

"What's happening?" said Mike. "I thought you were going to ask her."

"I did. She said yes. She put her hand on my shoulder."

Silence again. Images going through Jeffrey's mind, images very much alive and real. "Are you playing?" Mike asked.

"Yes. There's three girls playing with me. Alice, Susie and Cobby. I like Alice best. I want to wrestle with her but I'm not supposed to. Mrs. McCaferty would get mad. Look what Alice is doing – wiggling her nose as fast as she can. I'm giving her two bottles of milk. I put them in her hands real slowly. That way, I got to touch her each time."

"Do you like to touch Alice?"

"Yes. I told her I'll come back later with more milk. I have to go to Cobby now."

"Cobby can get her milk bottles later," Mike's voice said. "Nursery school is over for today. It's time to come back to the present, Jeffrey. But stay in a deep trance."

Jeffrey became slowly aware again of his body in the reclining chair, eyes still closed. Comfortable.

"Do you remember where you are now?" Mike asked him.

"Yes. With you and Jonathan in the hypnosis room."

"Do you remember having been with friends of yours in nursery school?"

"Sure."

"Do you remember Alice?"

"Of course."

"Well, tonight you are going to the mixer on campus, and you will meet Alice, all grown up."

"I will? I mean, I will. I will meet Alice."

"She may tell you her name is something else, but you'll know secretly that her real name is Alice. And you should call her Alice, no matter what she says. Do you understand?"

"Call her Alice. I understand."

"Tell Alice that you know her from nursery school. And remember – you like Alice very much. You've always liked her. You still want to touch her. You love her."

"I love her ..."

"And now I want you to forget everything that's happened in our session. When you wake up, you won't remember anything about reliving your experiences in nursery school, or that we talked about Alice. You now feel those memories of nursery school being covered over by a great white fog ... the white fog is rolling in, making you forget completely ..."

For Jeffrey, there was no evening that made him feel more uptight than Friday night. Fridays were usually when mixers were held. He'd had his fill of mixers his freshman year, but at an all-male school, there were very limited ways to socialize with members of the opposite sex. There were townies of course, mainly high school girls. Or you could go to Trenton or Newark and try to pick up girls, which usually ended in failure. For the mixers, girls were bussed in from near and far so they could have fun with some Ivy League studs. Those days, Jeffrey felt un-studly most of the time.

Jeffrey bundled up in his winter garb for the long, lonely walk up to the gym with his roommate Billy Bart. They didn't have much in common and rarely did things together. When it was freezing outside, Billy Bart would throw open the windows all the way, gulp cold air and complain that it was so hot and stuffy in their room that he couldn't stand it. And then Jeffrey would shiver and freeze, until he would get up nerve to go slam the windows shut. That's a good indication of what they had in common, and it often went downhill from there. But in spite of their sharp differences of opinion about what was hot and what was cold, they would often go to mixers together and then separate almost as soon as they went through the gymnasium doors.

From a distance, they could hear a band pounding out the beat. When they got inside, the music was deafening. Instead of leaping in and introducing himself to any girls, Jeffrey decided to stand against the wall for a while with his arms folded so he could practice playing it cool, like Jonathan did all the time.

The most embarrassing thing about a mixer was that just being there was a confession that you didn't have a date. Which in turn was a confession that there was something wrong with you, that you were basically unhappy.

Jeffrey knew how important it was to work up a smile at these affairs – and to hold onto it most of the evening. But in his present mood, he felt as if three smiles was probably the maximum he'd be able to manage all evening, and they would probably be somewhat brief. Quickies.

"Jeffrey, how're ya doing?" It was Ron Nash – Ron who had a top-secret black book with thirty girls on his 'cop a feel' list and ten others under the category of 'easy lay.'

"I'm doing real well," Jeffrey lied.

"Pretty good batch here tonight, huh?"

"I don't know," replied Jeffrey. "They look okay."

"Pretty good," Ron said, looking sharp in his Princeton blazer. "Unusual to see a batch this good." Then he got a little closer and talked in a lower voice. "See that one over there?"

"Which?"

"The one in the red dress. The cute one. I've got my eye on her. What do you think?"

"Not bad."

"She looks like a sure Q.F. to me," said Ron.

"Q.F.?"

"Quick Fuck. What's the matter, Jeffrey, you going senile? Hey, I hear you're working out at that research institute. Hypnotize any girls yet?"

"Not yet."

"Well, you ought to get on the stick! Hypnosis is supposed to work better than Spanish fly!"

"I don't know about that," said Jeffrey. "Say, what do you think of that one over there?"

"Not bad. WKOB – wouldn't kick her out of bed."

"I think I'll go see if she looks just as good close up."

"Go for it, Tiger!"

When Jeffrey got a few feet away, he decided he agreed with Ron Nash – he wouldn't kick her out of bed, either. As a matter of fact, there were probably very few girls Jeffrey would kick out of bed.

So there was nothing else to say but:

"Do you want to dance?"

At that point, one of two things can happen. Either she says yes, or she says no. If she says no, which Jeffrey pegged at a better than fifty-fifty chance, it means that she's already engaged or is seeing other guys – or that from the looks of you, you just aren't her kind of stuff.

She said yes. Jeffrey smiled. They got out on the dance floor, and he worked his body into a fit of gyration. She was sort of cute, with dark curly hair. She was definitely the kind of girl he could appreciate. He extended himself and used up smile number two, but she wasn't looking at him – she was staring at her feet, then at her swinging arms, then out into space.

He struck up a conversation.

"What's your name?"

"Leslie."

"My name's Jeffrey," he shouted. She couldn't hear him. "Jeffrey," he shouted again. She nodded her head as if to say, 'yeah, yeah, I heard you the first time.'

Then the music stopped, and it was that crucial time they had to decide whether or not to split up or stick together.

"What school do you go to, Alice?" he asked, hoping that she wouldn't give him a quick nod, turn her back and scamper for the hills. Not that there were any hills within a few miles.

"Douglass. I go to Douglass. And don't call me Alice."

"That's your name, isn't it, Alice?"

"What are you, nuts? I told you my name is Leslie."

"You sure it's not Alice? You look just like someone I knew named Alice."

"I've got a sister named Alice. I don't look anything like her."

"Did you ever go to a preschool in Washington, D.C.?"

"I'm from Connecticut," she said. "I've never been in D.C. Say, what time is it, anyway?"

He flipped out his watch. "It's ten-thirty."

"It's getting kind of late," she said.

She was right. In London, it was probably about four-thirty in the morning.

The band was playing again. Something nice and slow.

"C'mon, just one more. You've got time for one more dance, haven't you?"

He started dancing with her without waiting for her reply.

"Hey, watch it with the hands, Jeffrey."

"What's the matter?" he said.

"Just watch it."

On impulse, he kissed her. He had never done that before with a girl he'd just met. But he had a feeling that he and Alice were really old friends, and that they'd played together as kids.

"Okay, I really gotta go," she said, and stopped dancing.

"Aw, c'mon."

"No kiddin', I've got an exam tomorrow I haven't studied for. Besides, I'm not the kind of girl you think I am."

"What kind is that?"

"I'm not fast. And I don't like guys who are fast."

She started to back off, looking around for her coat.

Then poof.

She was gone.

Jeffrey felt queasy inside. It was always like this at mixers. The meaninglessness of life caught up with you, and inevitably you ended up with a lonely empty feeling in your gut. He wondered how many times he'd have to keep going through this routine until he melted away entirely.

Jeffrey during his early Princeton days with a backpack before he ditched the nerdy looking glasses and went with a style that was more John Lennon-esque / wire-rim

Jeffrey hitch-hiking in 1967, before growing his hair long

Witherspoon Hall, Jeffrey's Dormitory

7. Yab-Yum

Thanksgiving vacation was looming. Jonathan told Jeffrey of his non-plans to drive south in the MG with Pok, to head off and out with no itinerary just to see where the Zen path would lead them. Jeffrey concluded that, obviously, Jonathan hadn't resolved his conflict with his father because he wasn't heading to the California ranch for the holidays.

Before heading home himself, Jeffrey went shopping at Princeton's Army-Navy Store. A salesman who had a crewcut and looked like he was in ROTC waited on him.

"I'd like some boots, please," said Jeffrey.

"Certainly. What size do you wear?"

"I'm not exactly sure. We'd better measure."

He sat down and took off his pointy black lace-up shoes that made him look like a junior FBI agent. His mother had bought those shoes for him just before he'd left for college, and his mom had counted on those shoes lasting a whole year. He could just imagine what his mother would say when he arrived home for Thanksgiving wearing jeans, a work shirt and cowboy boots like Jonathan's. She'd say, "Boots, Jeffrey? Why boots?"

And sure enough, he was right.

"Boots don't become you," his mother said. "I can't imagine what possessed you to think you needed boots. Especially *that* type of boot. A *cowboy* boot? Really? Is that necessary?"

Over Thanksgiving, his parents both wondered what sort of questionable influences were taking their hold on him at college. He'd grown a subtle hint of sideburns, and his hair was down over his ears and almost reached to his collar. Long hair on men was fraught with political implications at the time. From a parental point of view, it was the symbol of the malcontents, the war protestors and, God forbid, the hippies. The change in his appearance was the subject of frequent conversations all vacation.

And so was the hypnosis research. They'd reluctantly succumbed to signing permission for him to be a hypnotic subject – he'd used every argument he could think of to win them over, the main one being his interest in psychology and what he might learn from the psychologists at the Institute. But his parents were suspicious about hypnosis, thinking it could throw Jeffrey off course. He spent half of Thanksgiving vacation defending Dr. Aaronson and Dr. Osmond, and trying to explain why it was okay that he had been assigned a hypnotist who had no medical training at all and who was merely an undergraduate psychology major. It was all a challenge, but Jeffrey had always been exceptional at debate.

The other half of vacation, when he wasn't eating turkey and stuffing, was spent sealed off in the family basement doing stop-motion animation for a new monster film. He had a sixteen-millimeter Bolex camera and last summer had built a two-foot-long rubber-skinned sea serpent with moveable joints. Using stop-motion techniques inspired by his favorite childhood film, 'The Seventh Voyage of Sinbad,' he was now making his sea serpent trample some of his old model railroad buildings.

It was a relief to get back to Princeton. And to top off his return, Jonathan phoned and invited him to lunch at Tower Club which Jonathan had joined at the beginning of his junior year. Jeffrey was overwhelmed when he saw how many campus celebrities belonged to that Eating Club – football players, sons of Congressmen, presidents of university societies. All the tables in the big dining room were stylishly prepared with attractive tablecloths. The situation looked like it probably had a hundred or two hundred years ago – with the waiters spooning clam chowder soup from a large bowl. Princeton was so rooted in Revolutionary War days that you half expected someone to scream out a warning: "The British are coming!"

Jonathan was in a somewhat somber mood. He right away interrogated Jeffrey about his vacation.

"My parents thought I'd changed a lot," said Jeffrey. "My mom especially doesn't like me wearing boots. And I had to put up with her harassment that I need a haircut. How about you? Did you have a good vacation?"

"It was really just perfect."

More food arrived – southern fried chicken with plantation-style cooking and service. The waiters at the club treated the students like royalty. Jeffrey was astonished to get this glimpse into upperclassman laid-back Eating Club life. He was used to eating at Commons, which resembled a military mess hall more than the splendor of dining on Prospect Street, also known as Eating Club Row.

Jeffrey told Jonathan about his latest monster movie and his long-harbored fantasies of a career in Hollywood producing something like another 'King Kong,' which in Jeffrey's mind, would rank as a truly noble achievement.

"Well," Jonathan told him, "from what I know about Hollywood, it's a crazy screwed-up life – dog eat dog, totally cutthroat. But if that's what you're really cut out for, why not? You only live once – until your next incarnation, anyway."

"My parents would kill me," Jeffrey explained. "Every time I even mention the movie business they begin a rant about how unstable that is, how nobody can make it unless you have family in the entertainment business. They think you need an M.D. or a Ph.D. to rank as anyone in this world. My Mom says I'd better keep making movies as a hobby."

"Doesn't sound like much support on the home front," said Jonathan. "There almost never is, for anybody."

"The best thing for me about Thanksgiving was getting to see my dog again."

"What kind of dog?" Jonathan asked.

"A beagle named Sandy. My sister and I have had him since he was a puppy."

"I've got a dog back home," said Jonathan. "He's half Australian Shepherd and half Dingo."

"Dingo?"

"Australian wild dog. So how was the mixer before the holidays? I've been curious to hear you tell me about it."

"Nothing special," said Jeffrey.

"Did you meet anyone?"

"Yeah, some girl."

"What was her name?"

"Uhm – Alice."

"You sure that was her name?"

"I'm not. I mean, she told me at first her name was Alice, then she said it was Leslie."

"Did you meet anyone at the mixer you'd met before?"

"Well, come to think of it, I thought I'd met Alice before, I had the strangest feeling that I knew her from way back. But she said she didn't remember me at all," Jeffrey explained.

"Do you remember anything about your last session right before Thanksgiving when Mike hypnotized you?"

"Not really. It's all foggy."

"Do you remember being age-regressed to nursery school?"

"Uhm – no."

"You don't remember playing milkman with a little girl named Alice when you were four years old?"

"Milkman? No."

"Well the reason you thought that girl's name was Alice was because Mike gave you a post-hypnotic suggestion to call her Alice. Mike's into that kind of control trip and Bernie does that kind of stuff all the time. I personally don't like it but it's a standard part of Humphry's research. Mike told you under hypnosis that you'd think that whatever girl you met at the mixer had been a friend of yours in nursery school. Is it coming back to you now?"

Jeffrey shook his head. He had zero recollection of it.

"Well, during our session this afternoon, I'll take you back into it and help you remember. But as you get deeper into hypnosis, there'll be more and more stuff you won't remember – especially when the training and first sessions are done, and I turn you over to Bernie to be your hypnotist. That's normal procedure, he does everything according to Humphry's original grant proposal. All subjects go through it."

Jonathan had put up some posters on the walls in the hypnosis cell. They made the room both more comfortable and more alluring. Jeffrey found one of them especially sexy – a black-on-white shadow picture of a man and woman sitting facing each other. The woman's naked breasts were silhouetted against the white background and she was sitting on the man's lap.

The title of the picture was 'Yab-Yum.' Jeffrey asked Jonathan what that meant.

"It's a Tibetan Tantric yoga pose, sexual yoga. I've got a book on it, you can borrow it if you want."

"You've, uhm, tried Yab-Yum?"

"Yeah," Jonathan confirmed.

"Linda said she does yoga."

"Hey, Linda does everything."

Jonathan lit incense, pulled a chair beside Jeffrey's recliner and started the induction, talking Jeffrey slowly down into trance, then saying Jeffrey's trance-induction word. In ten minutes Jeffrey was completely under, listening to Jonathan's voice but otherwise in a dreamless state of hypnotic sleep.

"Now I'm going to give you a suggestion, Jeffrey, which you will integrate for an hour or so into your personality when I wake you up. Then I'll bring you back down here and remove the condition. While you're awake under the condition, you won't remember that you've been hypnotized. You'll simply experience yourself and your environment as if it was natural – but there will be no past and no future. There will only be an eternal present which goes on forever. There will be no worries or anxieties from anything that happened in the past because there will be no past, and there will be no concern with the future because there will be no future. Do you understand?"

"Uhm," from the sleeping Jeffrey, "Yes, I understand."

"And one more important thing – during this 'eternal present' condition you will take on the personality of George Harrison. You will become the lead guitarist of the Beatles who just happens to be visiting this research institute. Do you understand?"

"George Harrison. Yes," said Jeffrey.

"Good. Now just relax ... let your mind become quiet, calm, silent ... breathe ... enjoy this eternal moment ... and as I count from five to one, you will slowly become more and more awake, so that when I reach the number 'one' you will wake up ... five ... you feel as if you are beginning to come out of a dream ... four ... slowly you are becoming conscious ... three ... you are beginning to wake up, starting to feel alert ... two ... you are almost ready to open your eyes and wake up, your breathing is waking up, you're beginning to feel your body in the chair ...

and now, when I clap my hands and say one, you will open your eyes and be totally awake. One!"

Jeffrey's eyes opened. He gazed around the room and focused on a poster of the Beatles.

"How do you feel?" Jonathan asked.

"Uhm, really good!"

"Do you remember your name?"

"Sure."

"What is it?"

Blankness for a moment – then – "Uh, George."

"So how are you liking it here in America, George?"

"Oh, jolly good. Jolly good indeed."

"What are you doing tomorrow morning?"

"Uhm, tomorrow. Let me see. I can't quite remember. Does it matter?"

"Not at all. Want to take a walk, have a tour of our place?"

"Sure, sounds great, jolly good."

"Okay, up you go!"

Jeffrey stood up. He felt slightly off-balance. "Let me see," he said, "where's my guitar?"

"I think Linda has it upstairs, shall we go up?"

"Who's Linda?"

"She's a chick who works here," Jonathan replied. "She's a big fan of yours, George. I promised her you'd give her your autograph before you caught your plane back to England to record your next album."

Jonathan led Jeffrey out of the hypnosis room and up the stairs. As they reached the hall on the main floor, Bernie came hurrying down.

"Bernie, I'd like you to meet George Harrison. He's visiting our research institute from England, he's the lead guitarist for the Beatles, you know, and he's interested in hypnosis."

"Very interesting," said Bernie, switching into the rules of the hypnotic condition. These kinds of things went on at the Institute every day of the week – that was why Pok had dubbed it the loony-bin. "Glad to meet you, Mr. Harrison."

They shook hands. "You can call me George," Jeffrey said.

"George it is then, great. Have a nice tour."

"I jolly well will."

"And Jonathan, come to my office when you're done."

Bernie continued down the hall.

"Nice chap," Jeffrey said. "But strange looking, isn't he? Like a leprechaun, the way he wobbles."

Linda was at her desk. "Linda, I'd like you to meet George Harrison," said Jonathan. "He's here for a short visit."

Standing up, she came around and extended her hand in a queenly gesture. Jeffrey took it gallantly.

"Jolly nice skirt you've got on there," said Jeffrey, glancing at her legs. "Nice blouse too. I like girls who wear that kind. It exposes quite a bit, wouldn't you say?"

"Do you like what you see?"

"Oh yes, quite."

"So you're really the famous George Harrison? I've always wanted to meet you!"

"Flattered, to be sure," said Jeffrey.

"Do you think I'm as pretty as all your English girls?"

"No comparison, you're even prettier."

"Well now I am flattered." She grinned and posed seductively with her hip off to one side. "You make me embarrassed," she said. "You have such penetrating eyes – as if you can see right through my clothes. You excite me."

"Well don't get too excited. It's bad for the digestion."

Linda laughed. "Could I get your autograph?" she asked.

"Of course."

She went over to her desk and got a Magic Marker.

"Where would you like me to sign?"

"Well I was thinking, maybe, if you don't mind of course, somewhere really personal. How about right here?"

She pulled up her skirt, swung her leg up onto the desk and pointed to a spot right below her pink underwear. Jeffrey grinned, placed one hand on her naked thigh for leverage and started to write. "G...E...O...R...G...E."

"It's time we were on our way to the airport, George," said Jonathan, twenty minutes later. "Your plane leaves for London in two hours. And we have to get your overcoat. You left it in the basement."

"I don't remember wearing an overcoat."

"Sure you did."

When they re-entered the hypnosis cell, Jeffrey protested. "I don't see any overcoat here."

"Don't worry about that, George, just have a seat for a moment in that reclining chair."

"I thought we came down here for my coat."

But Jeffrey sat down nevertheless.

"Just close your eyes, push the chair back, there, atta boy, now just listen to my voice while you breathe deeply, good, very deep breaths, a good sigh ... you're relaxing, feeling the pull of gravity on your body ..."

It was some time later that Jeffrey opened his eyes and he was Jeffrey again. Jonathan had given him a complete memory block as per his specified instructtions for this training session, erasing all recollection of the hypnotic condition from consciousness.

"So how do you feel?" Jonathan asked him.

"Uhm – relaxed."

"What do you remember of the last hour or so?"

"Well, I remember you sitting there starting to hypnotize me. I remember closing my eyes. I guess I went to sleep. And – did I talk to Linda?"

Jonathan was surprised that Jeffrey was able to recall that detail of the session. In a completely trained subject – a subject ready to work with Bernie on the actual test conditions – every memory of having seen Linda would have been blanked out.

"You did talk to Linda for a while. Do you remember what you said?"

"No."

"Did you do anything special when you saw her?"

"Uhm – no. Did I ask her to the Harvard Game?"

"I don't know – did you?"

"I don't think so," said Jeffrey.

"Maybe you should. I'll bet she'd be up for it."

Jeffrey at last with long hair (left) and Jonathan (right) soaking in some rays side by side

Jonathan on the family ranch in Ojai, California

Princeton's Alexander Hall, where Timothy Leary once lectured

Firestone Library, Princeton University

8. The Great Iron Gates

Jonathan was standing in front of the great iron gates of Princeton University, a little nervous, a little cold. He'd had two dates with Anne since their blind date. Both times he'd met her in New York. He wondered how she would feel about being on the campus again – whether the magic of their first meeting would still be 'blowin' in the wind.' When he thought back to that evening, the main thing he remembered was the graceful wild-animal way she'd swayed to Brahms.

In New York they'd spent a lot of time focused on horses, which he'd loved. But sexually they both seemed surprisingly shy, as if they had all their lives to explore each other at that level, quietly indulging in the slightest touch and simplest kiss. What he was beginning to suspect was that he was in fact really finally falling in love with somebody and this was how it was naturally unfolding.

There was also the slight nausea that struck when things got hot and abated when he eased up. Something was going on but each time he tried to think about it, his mind got blurry and distracted. Now, waiting for the bus, he could feel his sexual charge wanting finally to push through bashfulness and nausea and all the rest, her return to Princeton had him feeling both nervous and excited – he admitted to himself that Anne reminded him of his mother and he told himself, well –so what?

The bus finally approached, undaunted by stray cars and dodging pedestrians. The New York smell of Diesel reminded

Jonathan of the John Deere tractor back home – scent of nostalgia from across the continent, departed past arriving with the present.

The bus came to a stop in front of the mob of students who were standing around waiting for their dates. The doors popped open and girls started pouring out – Friday night load from Vassar, Smith, Douglass and elsewhere. He watched their faces as they emerged. Confident, not too open, smiling the prep-school smile, laughing the coed laugh. Something about it seemed unreal – weekend relationships for four years with no continuity. The whole scene made Jonathan dizzy.

And then he saw them, the two guys in suits who'd lectured him at the parking lot – they were standing just fifteen feet from him, just casually standing there as if waiting for some bus but actually standing there so that he could see them standing there watching him.

The two men tipped their hats, turned and walked onto the campus, heading in the direction of Alexander Hall. Jonathan recalled that Alexander Hall was where Timothy Leary had given a speech at Princeton – a speech that was supposed to have been mainly about psychology and the Leary Personality Profile Test, but the speech had quickly turned to focus heavily on psychedelic drugs and the meaning of Timothy Leary's new favorite slogan: 'Turn On, Tune In and Drop Out.' Jonathan suddenly had a flash memory of an Institute party that Timothy Leary had attended the evening after the lecture. He recalled Dr. Leary being very high at that party as he had spouted endlessly about his League for Spiritual Discovery up at a vast estate in Millbrook, New York. The estate had been donated by Peggy Hitchcock, a member of the very wealthy Mellon family, famous for their art galleries and philanthropic activities. Timothy Leary had suggested that Jonathan visit Millbrook sometime, a place that all the hippie and beatnik intellectuals, including beat poet Allan Ginsberg, were turning into their second home. "We have a watch tower where somebody is always high on acid twenty-four hours a day," Timothy Leary had explained, "and a lake where everyone likes to swim naked when the weather is fine."

Suddenly Jonathan snapped out of his memories as he realized that there were no more female faces coming from the interior of the bus, in fact the bus was beginning to move away and where was Anne? Everyone was leaving the bus stop with their dates but Jonathan was left standing there alone. She hadn't come. Either she'd missed the bus out of New York, or she'd just forgotten.

"Jonathan?"

He turned around. She was standing behind him, laughing. "Hey," he said, "how'd you get off without me seeing you?" She looked real good – cheeks flushed, ears muffed.

"You were so busy eyeing all the other girls, it was easy," she joked.

He picked up her suitcase.

"So how have you been?" she asked, taking his other hand.

"Oh – getting by. Been a long week with classes, fencing, the Institute."

"It feels good to be out of the city."

"How about a cup of coffee before we go to the dorm?"

"Sure."

Henderson's was crowded but they found a table in the back away from the counter and the noise. Jonathan ordered coffee, Anne ordered tea.

"I have a fencing practice at the gym in awhile," said Jonathan. "I'd like to skip it but Coach has been down on me lately for missing so many practices. Want to come watch?"

"I'd love to see you fence."

"Can you stay the whole weekend?"

"I can stay until Sunday morning," she said. She dipped her tea-bag into the hot water and then gently lifted it out again. "Sunday afternoon I have a date for a concert."

"Oh."

She poured the tea into her cup. "I hope you don't mind."

He shrugged his shoulders. Why should he mind?

"Do you?" she asked.

"Course not."

"I could cancel it if you want. My date is just someone Rachael set me up with a couple weeks ago. It's just that they're going to be performing Beethoven's Pastoral Symphony. I've never had a chance to hear it in concert."

"No sense in passing up an opportunity like that."

The three o'clock bells were ringing from Nassau Hall as they headed down to the dorm. Most of the way they walked in silence. Winter beginning. Cold but no wind. Premonitions of snow and the smell of fireplace smoke. They left Anne's suitcase in Jonathan's dorm and then headed down to the gym.

Anne watched the basketball team practice on the main floor while Jonathan went down to the locker room to suit up, and then they went upstairs to the fencing balcony together. Ever since Jonathan had been a kid back on the ranch he'd been fascinated by sword fighting. Whenever there'd been a break down at the corrals working cattle, he and his brothers used to take their dad's bullwhips and use them for sword fighting. Jonathan had read *The Three Musketeers* about twenty times. When he arrived at Princeton and discovered that they had fencing as a regular sport, he'd joined the freshman team right away.

Up until the beginning of this academic year, he'd been Coach's most devoted disciple, almost father and son. Among the fencing coaches in the Ivy League, Stan Sieja was known as the best. He'd been on Poland's winning Olympic team in days gone by and was a master at strategy – when it came to planning intricate attacks against a known opponent, he was fantastic. But recently Jonathan was becoming more and more certain that there was more to fencing than perfect technique. Coach's approach was so mathematically precise and structured that it left no room for spontaneous impulse or innovation – but for over a year now Jonathan's main interest in fencing had been in the Zen approach that Pok had told him about – the method of the Samurai warriors of ancient Japan who considered strategy and preprogrammed attacks ultimately secondary to spontaneity.

However, every time Jonathan tried to fence the way he had read the Samurai warriors did – to move beyond thinking about technique and just to get out on the mat and quiet the mind and fence without forethought – Coach would come down on his back like a grammar school teacher rapping a disobedient student's knuckles.

Tod Mendelsohn was leading both the freshman and varsity teams in jumping jacks as Anne and Jonathan entered the indoor fencing balcony. Everyone was lined up in six uniform rows, jumping in unison as if they were in the army. It was against regulations to bring dates to practice, so Jonathan figured he'd better get an okay from Coach for Anne to watch the workout. As they walked toward Coach's office, he could feel forty pairs of horny eyes checking out Anne's bod.

Coach was talking on the phone, so they went over and sat down on the sofa against the far wall. The office was a mess as usual – electric epées on the bench waiting to be repaired, helmets dented from sabre attacks, electric scoring equipment piled in the corner by the window. Everything was always in a mess but everything was always ready for tournaments. Good old European discipline underneath it all. Finally Coach ended his conversation and came over to them.

"I'd like you to meet a good friend of mine," said Jonathan, standing up and introducing Anne.

"It's a pleasure to meet such a lovely young lady," Coach said in his Polish accent, giving her his winning smile. Coach was over fifty but he still loved to flirt with dates.

"Anne's from San Francisco," said Jonathan, just to let him know that she wasn't some Vassar wench.

"But I'm living in New York now," she said.

"She's never seen any fencing before," Jonathan explained, "so do you mind if she watches practice today?"

"Well, we have some very important meets coming up. We must win them if we're going to take the Ivy League title again this year, right, Jonathan?"

Same old dig.

"Right, Coach."

"But I think we could make an exception to the rule just this once, Anne, and let you watch." Another winning smile.

"Thank you," she said, and smiled back.

"I guess I'd better get out and warm up," Jonathan said, heading for the door. He expected Anne to come with him, but Coach offered to take her coat and then started to chat with her, so Jonathan went out onto the fencing floor alone.

Tod was leading the calisthenics as if it were an enormous responsibility. Practice was set up on a rigid schedule – so long for this, so long for that. Ten minutes of jogging, twenty minutes of warm-up exercises, ten minutes of lunges and ten minutes of going through blade work exercises in pairs. Then there were some actual bouts, round-robins where everyone fenced everyone else. Jonathan half-heartedly did the exercises and watched the other fencers working themselves as hard as they could. One, two, three, four, stretch those muscles, flex those toes. After three years, the routine got boring. Jesus – maybe Bernie was right, thought Jonathan – maybe fencing was a waste of time.

Finally they broke up into their respective weapon groups: foil, epée and sabre. After Jonathan worked out for a few minutes with one of the other foil men, Tod came over and asked him if he had a moment to talk. Tod was always into his role as captain, taking fencers aside and talking over new attack paradigms he'd learned from Coach. Jonathan was glad he'd turned down the captain's position and let Tod have it. Tod had short hair and bright brains and a promising future as long as he played all the right games and didn't ask too many questions – good material for a leader. Still, Jonathan regretted that he'd missed being the first 'Zen Hypnotist Captain of the Princeton Fencing Team.'

Jonathan took off his helmet and leaned on his sword. "So what's on your mind?" he asked Tod.

"Well, Coach and I had a long talk yesterday when you didn't show up for practice again," Tod began. So that was it. "Coach is really starting to get upset –"

"Look, Tod, I had to work late at the Institute yesterday. I've got an important commitment out there, you know."

"You also have an important commitment to the team."

"I win, don't I?"

"That's not the point."

"So what is the point?"

"It's a matter of spirit. Team spirit. You're about the best foil man Coach has ever trained. You have every chance in the world of coming out number one in the nation this year, of placing Princeton at the top."

"So?"

"Well, Coach is naturally upset. He just can't understand the change that's come over you in the last year."

"What change? What's he so upset about?"

"It's your attitude."

"My attitude toward what?"

"Your attitude toward the team, you just don't seem to care about us anymore. You're the champion of all the younger fencers, they look up to you as their hero. The example you set affects everyone – what you do, they imitate. You're in psychology, you should understand that."

"Wait just a minute. What I do, I do. I'm into fencing my own way, and if you don't like it, there's nothing I can do to help you."

Tod gave Jonathan a long stare that Jonathan supposed was intended to make him feel guilty. Tod seemed to be learning Coach's manipulation techniques pretty well.

"Look, Tod, you're doing the best you can the only way you know how, and I'm doing the best I can, the only way I know. So come on, why don't we just fence, okay? I didn't come to practice today to argue philosophy."

Tod lowered his helmet.

Jonathan did the same.

Jonathan tried to relax and get into his Zen-fencing state of mind, not trying to win, just attempting to stay centered, totally aware of the present. Suddenly Tod made a fleche attack, jabbing his blade right into Jonathan's crotch as he ran by him. Jonathan told him, goddamnit, watch your fucking point, and Tod replied that Jonathan had parried him too low.

They backed off and went at it again. Jonathan held his ground, kept his cool. When the Zen electricity hit, he lunged and touched Tod cleanly on the chest. He got two more touches but then suddenly lost the Zen flash and had to go back to fencing with Coach's European techniques in order to win. Hopefully by the time the championships arrived, he'd have perfected his Zen technique so that the flash would last the whole meet. If he could defeat last year's National Foil Champion with his Zen method, he could beat anybody. And then Coach would have to admit that the simple meditative ways of the ancient East were superior to all the calculated strategies of the modern technological West.

The scene at Tower Club was noisy as usual, everyone had dates for the Harvard Game and nearly everyone was drunk. Before dinner, Jonathan and Anne went upstairs to the Tube-Room to watch superstar newsman Walter Cronkite and his up-to-the-minute Vietnam War flicks. Nothing like a little military inspiration from the front. The TV room was filled with the sound of exploding bombs and strafing jets. Cronkite was showing a squadron of U.S. planes napalming a Viet Cong stronghold. Watching real people getting killed had become regular nightly fare on TV, but for Jonathan it always evoked an almost violent reaction because of what had happened to his big brother in 'Nam.

By the time they went down to dinner, Jonathan was in a mute mood. "What is it, what are you thinking about?" Anne asked him quietly.

"What?" he muttered, glancing up from his food.

"The news seemed to really upset you," she pointed out.

"Oh – that. We shouldn't have even gone into the TV room when the news was on, I always get angry."

"Yeah, pretty depressing, the war in Vietnam."

"My brother, he was a conscientious objector but they sent him to 'Nam as a psychiatric assistant anyway. He had to fly off and land in a helicopter in the jungle and try to get the guys who freaked out under fire back to the chopper before they got shot. He came back from all that last year totally knocked flat inside. He told me that the war was entirely unjust – but I'm sure you heard my classmates up there cheering when we bombed a Vietnamese village – innocent women and children – in the name of freedom and peace."

"I hope you don't get drafted, Jonathan."

He nodded a very pensive nod. "One way or another I'll never go over there."

After dinner they decided to catch the nine o'clock movie at the Princeton Playhouse – some old W.C. Fields films. Top intellectual fare for our nation's budding eggheads. Jonathan had seen the show a few nights before with Pok but he was up for a second performance.

Halfway through one of the W.C. Fields features, Anne snuggled up against Jonathan's shoulder and he put his arm around her. When the program ended they stayed seated while everybody else left. Then they stood up and Anne put her hand lightly on Jonathan's arm as they made their exit.

Feeling a bit exhausted and a touch nauseous, Jonathan took Anne over to the Princeton Inn where she had a reservation. Men weren't allowed into the girls' hotel rooms after nine o'clock in the evening – one of the typical Victorian regulations of Princeton township. But she came against him and kissed him longer and deeper than ever before, pressing her body tightly against his just for a moment ...

When Jonathan got back to the dorm everything was quiet and the lights were off. It was almost one in the morning, the herd bedded down for the night. Jonathan sat down on his couch in his room to inspect a nail that was coming through the heel of his boot. He pulled off his other boot and then opened his window and stepped out onto the ledge.

He saw a solitary girl walking below him on the path. Suddenly he felt so light he felt as if he could fly – swoop down and take her off to Peter Pan's hideaway. Pok was right, he thought – a glider up here would be just the thing. They could make the leap and soar across the quad like birds.

Something started coming back into his mind – a hypnotic condition Bernie had given Jonathan to become a dove. He'd suddenly experienced himself not in his human body but actually within the body of a dove. He remembered flapping his wings in the basement of the Institute, taking off and flying out of the room along the corridor, searching for open air – up the stairs, over Linda's head and then right out the open front door ... and into freedom. Damnit, what had happened then? He'd flown away and he'd never returned – somehow he was still out there as a dove, flying around forever ...

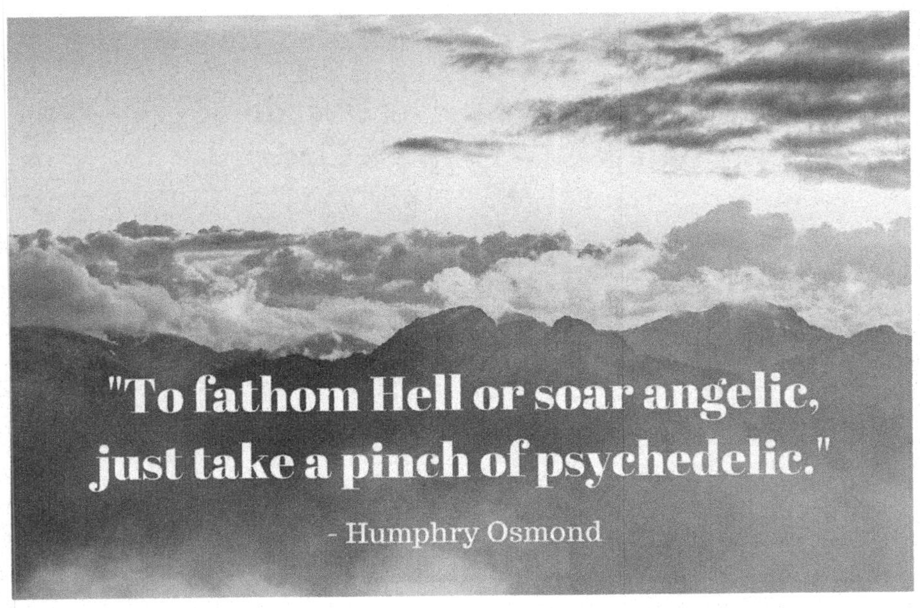

Humphry Osmond . . . drug pioneer

Mind Control Study Continued for Decade After CIA Said It Was Ended, Book Claims

BY NORMAN KEMPSTER
Times Staff Writer

WASHINGTON—The CIA sponsored scientific research into methods of controlling the human mind for almost a decade after it ended its previously disclosed experiments with LSD in 1963, author John Marks says in a new book

Citing documents released by the agency under the Freedom of Information Act, Marks, a former State Department intelligence officer, said the CIA continued at least until mid-1972 to search for exotic ways to dominate the brain and control behavior

Ultimately, the agency admitted that its experimentation, which began in 1950 in the midst of the cold war, was a failure—the human mind was either too resilient or too unpredictable to be molded with the reliability required for espionage operations.

The book, "The Search for the 'Manchurian Candidate,'" quotes a CIA document as saying that the mind-control programs finally ended July 10, 1972, when the chief of the project, Dr. Sidney Gottlieb, wrote its bureaucratic epitaph.

"The Clandestine Service has been able to maintain contact with the leading edge of developments in the field of biological and chemical control of human behavior," Gottlieb wrote. "It has become increasingly obvious over the last several years that this general area had less and less relevance to current clandestine operations . . . .

"On the scientific side, it has become very clear that these materials and techniques are too unpredictable in their effect on individual human beings, under specified circumstances, to be operationally useful. Our operations officers . . . have shown a discerning and perhaps commendable distaste for utilizing these materials and techniques."

The materials and techniques included LSD and a wide variety of mind-altering drugs, sexual entrapment, electric shock, electrodes implanted in the brain, radiation and hypnosis. The program was conducted under such code names as Bluebird, Artichoke, MK-ULTRA, MK-NAOMI, MK-SEARCH and Project Often.

The objectives were to develop a foolproof truth serum to be used in questioning agents, defectors and enemy prisoners; to determine if brainwashing was possible; to devise ways of producing amnesia so that agents could not disclose secrets if captured; and to develop a variety of ways of killing and incapacitating enemies.

It was once the CIA's deepest secret. The public did not get its first glimpse of the mind control program until 1975, when a commission headed by then-Vice President Nelson A. Rockefeller reported that an Army civilian employe—since identified as Dr. Frank Olson—had committed suicide in 1953 after having been given LSD without his knowledge.

The Rockefeller report provided no details, but in the last three years additional information has seeped out. In his book, Marks pulls the story together, showing for the first time its scope, placing previous disclosures in context and filling in some of the blanks.

For example, he reports that in the 1960s Dr. James Hamilton, a San Francisco psychiatrist, received CIA funds to conduct "clinical testing of behavioral control materials" on inmates at the California Medical Facility at Vacaville. Although the records do not indicate the precise nature of the experiments, they show that in 1967 and 1968 Hamilton spent more than $10,000 in CIA funds to pay volunteers. At prison pay scales, that means he probably experimented on between 400 and 1,000 inmates.

Marks says that in the late 1950's the CIA paid some—although not all—of the expenses of Dr. Ewen Cameron's unorthodox psychological programs at a hospital in Montreal. Cameron used massive electric shock treatments combined with long periods of sleep in an effort to "depattern" schizophrenic patients.

According to Marks, the CIA's interest in LSD in the early 1950's created much of the international market for the drug. Marks speculates that without CIA experiments—most of them carried out on college campuses—the drug-oriented counterculture of the 1960's might never have started.

9. The Light of Reason Fails

Jonathan woke up Saturday morning into one of those rare moments in eternity when mundane reality is transformed for a brief flash and the Muses can be seen laughing in the ether. Homer and Lao Tzu and Socrates and Cervantes and Shelley and Shakespeare all singing in harmony together to bring up the sun.

But before rolling out of bed, he remembered the night before and the flashback of becoming a dove – and then he glanced at the pile of books and research papers on his worn oak floor and remembered a research report on the Institute he'd copied without permission. Even though he was now officially on staff, he still wasn't allowed access to hush-hush Top Secret stuff about the Institute's research – but he wanted to know everything, and he felt he had earned the right to find out. The report didn't tell it all, by any means, but at least it offered a few clues.

The day before yesterday he'd read it quickly. It contained a lot of information that had been withheld from him when he was a hypnotic subject. Now he got out of bed naked in the chill, picked it up and turned to the part about hypnosis projects: Report of Research Activities, Department of Experimental Psychology, N.J.N.P.I.

"The research program of the Section of Experimental Psychology continues to focus on the effects of perception on behavior. At the present time, new non-drug methods for producing altered states of awareness are being assessed. The major focus of study continues to be the effects of hypnotically induced perceptual changes on behavior. An examination of the effects of perceived increased gravity and decreased gravity has been introduced and compared with the effects of increased and decreased strength. Under increased gravity subjects showed many of the same reactions as with decreased strength – in both cases the subjects felt sick. In the decreased gravity and increased strength conditions, the subjects became happy, active and energetic. This was especially marked under the decreased gravity condition ..."

Jonathan's thoughts began racing. When Bernie had hypnotized him and turned him into a dove, he had been free of gravity – he had flown. The report said that decreased gravity made subjects happy, active and energetic. That was true, it had been a happy feeling at first, a sensation of total freedom. In fact, that had been the only time since he had become a hypnotic subject that he had felt totally free of the Institute and all the other hassles in his life. Perhaps that had been part of the reason for his happiness – he had flown away and left all his cares and worries behind. But then things had become frightening, mostly because of the fog – he'd become lost in the fog and hadn't been able to find his way.

He could vaguely remember trying to call out to Bernie for help, to show him the way back, but Bernie hadn't brought him back, he was sure of that – Bernie had led him somewhere ... to some strange place where weird things had happened – then Bernie had blotted out the memory of flying away as a dove and had awakened him from the trance. But he had felt more real being inside the body of the dove ...

He put the research report down, went over to his stereo and turned on the amplifier. Richard Farina's second album was still on the turntable.

The music started softly – a combination of American Bluegrass and early English Ballad:

"Now is the time for your loving dear
And the time for your company
Now when the light of reason fails
And the fires burn on the sea
Now in this age of confusion
I have need for your company."

Truer words were never spoken, he thought, dialing the Princeton Inn to see if Anne was awake. They connected him to her room and she answered the phone right away. She offered to walk over and meet him at his dorm but he said no, he'd be right there, he needed the exercise.

He jogged all the way to the Princeton Inn. Anne was waiting outside. They didn't kiss but he could tell she was feeling as good as he now was, being in her company again. They headed up to the Annex to meet Pok for breakfast. When they arrived at the restaurant, Pok was waiting outside the front door playing his harmonica. He gave Anne a courtly bow and tipped his invisible hat, doing his Charlie Chaplin routine.

Anne laughed and Pok kept up his pantomime routine as they went inside, down the stairs, through the heavy doors and into the Annex, one of the best restaurants on Nassau Street. A waitress showed them to a table, a booth over in the corner with a white tablecloth and a red candle.

"So you're living in Sodom I hear," Pok said to Anne, finally dropping his mute act.

"For the last few months," said Anne.

"Well, we'll let you know before we spike the water."

"What?"

"Pok thinks that the only cure for New York is the acid cure," Jonathan explained. "A little psychedelic mouthwash to clear up the bad breath of over-urbanization."

"Ah. Oh. Where are you from, Pok?"

"Kicked off the reservation. Princeton's token Arapaho. Actually my mom's Indian but my dad's Greek. I grew up pretty much all over the world which is why I'm so socially maladjusted – I never knew the blissful joys of suburbia."

They ordered omelets. Pok retrieved a bottle of wine from his backpack and opened it with his corkscrew. Like Gnossos Pappadopoulis, the maladjusted hero in one of their all-time favorite books, Richard Farina's *Been Down So Long It Looks Like Up To Me*, Pok carried around all his essential survival equipment in his backpack – which included wine plus a sizeable quantity of smoking contraband.

"Wine for breakfast?" said Jonathan.

"Don't look at me, the French invented the custom."

They finished their water and Pok poured wine into the empty glasses. "I'd like to propose a toast," he said. "May the seeds of negative karma fall from the vine of life onto stony ground, thereupon to rot and decay so that the white light may reach us unhindered from a distant astral realm."

"Hear hear," said Jonathan.

"And to my sex life," Pok added. "That it may dramatically improve."

They clinked glasses.

"Pok's chick split the scene," Jonathan explained. "He's still riding the tail end of the bummer."

"Why did she leave?" Anne asked him.

"I chased her away," said Pok. "She vapor-locked, blew her cool and flew the coop to Mexico. As they say, ashes to ashes, dust to dust. Chicks come and chicks go."

"Why did you chase her away?"

"Where did you find this lady, Jonathan?" asked Pok. "She asks such illuminating questions! I've been reflecting on that for many a moment now, and my only reply is – I was following a hypnotic command."

"Are you for real?" Jonathan retorted, hearing this for the first time.

"I think it was a going-away present from the Institute before I was relieved of my subject duties – a condition to split up with Shana. Maybe they figured that if Shana hit the bricks, I'd come back like a loyal pup, hanging my head in shame for straying from the hypnotic path." Pok downed more wine. "Weird things have been coming back – I remember more and more what they did to me."

Just then their omelets came and were soon consumed. Anne excused herself to use the ladies' room.

"Far-out chick," said Pok when she was out of earshot. "Let me know when you're trading her in. You balling her yet?"

"Jesus Christ, Pok."

"More coffee?" It was the waitress. They were holding up the table. They said no, she handed Jonathan the bill and Pok gallantly stole it away and slipped off to the cash register.

Pok vanished after breakfast, saying he had to visit a sick friend. The Harvard game wasn't until two, so after spending an hour or so walking around the campus and browsing in some of the shops on Nassau Street, Jonathan and Anne stopped by a delicatessen and bought the makings of a picnic lunch. They found the MG where Pok had last left it, put the top down and drove out into the country.

Jonathan knew a dirt road that went to a meadow which was far enough away from campus that no one would bother them. They drove to the end of the road and walked up the hillside until they found a grassy spot overlooking the valley. Spreading out the blanket, they relaxed side by side. Noon approached and they feasted. Wine avec popping cork, corned beef sandwiches on rye, cheese cut with his pocket knife and grapes from South Africa – the big, dark solid ones that you can roll around in your mouth for hours.

They ate until they were stuffed and the bottle of wine was almost empty. "You keep drifting off to someplace that seems to bother you," Anne said after a long silence.

Jonathan was hesitant a moment. Then he spoke up.

"Last night when I got back to my room, I had a hypnotic flashback. It happens to me sometimes. I don't have much control over it when in happens."

"What was it like?" she asked.

"It was about being a dove – one of the conditions Bernie gave me last spring. I have a really strange memory of becoming a dove under hypnosis and flying away somewhere. The trouble is, I don't have a clear memory of ever coming back. I know Bernie woke me up from that condition, but I still have a weird feeling that part of me flew away and I'll never be able to find the missing part. Does that sound totally weird?" He glanced at her, hoping for understanding.

"Tell me more," she said.

"At one point last spring, when I was doing hypnosis sessions three times a week, suddenly everything went completely out of focus in my head. I got so confused Wayne and Glen took me to the infirmary for a checkup. The shrink I saw at the Infirmary, Dr. Dalrymple, said I should quit being a subject at the Institute and start therapy at the Infirmary, but Bernie advised me against it, so I told the shrink that I didn't believe any of that Mumbo-Jumbo Freudian stuff."

"You stayed at the Institute after that experience?"

"I have a lot at stake out there – like my draft deferment that Bernie keeps promising me if I stay on to work for him after I graduate. And then there are all the professional opportunities that come along with being a research hypnotist. And anyway, along with the freaky parts I've also had a lot of good times at the Institute." He paused for a moment. A bird landed a few feet from him, looked quizzically at them, then took off again.

"Maybe that was your missing part," said Anne to lighten their mood – and it worked. Jonathan relaxed, yawned, took her hand and kissed it as though she were a princess.

"It's good you tell me these things," she said.

"I feel I can trust you."

"We don't really need a football game, do we? Why don't we just stay here, talk and relax all afternoon?"

"Great idea," he said, grinning.

Just then a breeze picked up, bending the dry grass in rustling waves as it played across the meadow. A cloud momentarily obscured the sun and there was a foreboding of winter in the sudden shade. Then the sun came out again.

"Ah, the sun's so warm," Anne intoned. "And I'm feeling free like your dove. Would it be entirely safe and okay if I took off my blouse or would that be, I don't know, overly promiscuous?"

"Nobody ever comes out here."

And so she did, just like that.

A736
$2.95
PSYCHEDELICS
by Bernard Aaronson
and
Humphry Osmond

10. Praise of Old Nassau

Jeffrey and Linda stood in line for hotdogs, then walked up the cement stairs and emerged into sunlight. There it was, the Coliseum – the brightness of green turf surrounded by a multitude of cheering drinking fun-time fans. They found their seats – not especially good seats, but the best Jeffrey could muster as a sophomore.

The game began with a great kickoff. Everybody stood up and roared as the players exploded into skull-cracking action. Jeffrey spent half the game watching the field and the other half sneaking glances at Linda's mammary bounces under her tight sweater.

"I just love football," she exclaimed at one point, just as he was watching her bounce. "Have you been to many games?"

"Almost every one," he replied, breathless.

"Do you always have a date?"

"Not always," he said.

"I'll bet you have girlfriends at half the schools in the Ivy League."

"What do you take me for, a lecherous Playboy?"

"Well, certainly an aspiring Playboy. And lecherous? You haven't come out of the closet yet, but there's potential."

They were both crushed when Princeton lost 14 to 17 in a last-minute field goal by Harvard. All the alumni stood up afterwards to sing "In Praise of Old Nassau," the official Princeton alma mater song:

"Tune every harp and every voice,
Bid every care withdraw,
Let all with one accord rejoice,
In Praise of Old Nassau.
In Praise of Old Nassau, my boys,
Hoorah, Hoorah, Hoorah,
Her sons will give
While they shall live,
Three cheers for Old Nassau."

And so forth ... finally, once everyone who remembered the words to all seven verses finished singing, the crowd headed out of the stadium to drown their sorrows. Linda walked close beside Jeffrey, sharing the gloom of defeat. Jeffrey was all the more depressed because Ron Nash had predicted Princeton would lose, and they'd made a bet on it and now Jeffrey owed Ron a case of Budweiser.

They had dinner at an Italian restaurant in town. Linda played footsies with Jeffrey underneath the table. And with her light, tongue-in-cheek banter she played footsies with him above the table too.

"I still can't understand why you want to be a psychiatrist, Jeffrey," she said. "You don't seem the type at all."

"What type do I seem like?"

"Do you play guitar?"

"Nope. Just clarinet."

"Too bad. That pretty much rules out becoming a music superstar, unless you can play like Benny Goodman or Pete Fountain."

"Not even close," Jeffrey confessed.

"How about heading for Hollywood?"

"Hollywood? That's not a bad idea. I could probably have a booming psychotherapy practice there."

"Psychotherapy practice? What are you talking about? I was thinking you should be an actor. Like Jimmy Stewart. He was from Princeton, wasn't he?"

"Uhm, yeah."

"If you were in the movies, Jeffrey, would you rather be a hero in war movies, or a great lover?"

"Uhm, neither," said Jeffrey, grinning. "I'd be the guy they cast as the monster – like in 'I Was a Teenage Werewolf.'

"That would be good casting," she said. "You are quite a wolf, Jeffrey. I'll bet you don't realize that yet, do you?"

"I actually made a werewolf movie once. Leon, this friend of mine in high school, volunteered to lay down on the floor while I applied hairs to his face a few frames at a time, using latex. When you run the movie at full speed, it looks like he's really turning into one of the hairiest werewolves you've ever seen. I played the film director trying to make the werewolf stay put, but in the story he escapes. That's actually the only film footage I have of myself and it's really short. About ten seconds of me jumping up and down shouting at the werewolf – and it's a silent film."

"Well you should have been the werewolf," said Linda. "You're such a devil."

"Yeah, but in real life nobody goes out to Hollywood to actually make monster movies."

"Some people do."

"Yeah, but not Ivy League students whose parents expect them to go to medical school to become a psychiatrist."

After dinner they drove in Linda's old car to the nearby town of Hopewell where she lived. Jeffrey had a secret plan for getting to first base with her that very night. Little did he suspect that Linda's own game plan was to have him hit as many home runs as he could before he passed out from exaustion.

After twenty minutes of playing verbal footsies in her tiny living room, she led him into her bedroom to let him try out the waterbed. He sat down hesitantly, feeling nervous about opportunity appearing so close at hand. He was finally alone with a seductive, warm, bouncy, effervescent girl (admittedly several years his senior) who seemed up for making out – but he had no idea how to get started without making his intent seem overly obvious.

"By the way, Jeffrey, did you remember to bring any rubbers?"

Jeffrey gasped. "Uh, rubbers? Uh, gee, no, I didn't."

"Don't worry, my period just ended yesterday," she told him. "There's no way I could get pregnant."

"Oh – uh – I'm sure glad – good."

All the practice in the world hadn't adequately prepared Jeffrey for this moment of truth. He could take all those Playboy magazines and chuck them for all the help they provided. And all of Ron Nash's coaching and instructional bull-rap-sessions proved equally worthless, the moment Linda started undoing Jeffrey's belt.

"We shouldn't be doing this, you know," said Jeffrey, but then remembered that that was usually the girl's line.

"Why not? Are you feeling uptight?"

"Me? Uptight? No. It's just that –"

"Go ahead, say it. You're not attracted to me."

"I am, really. It's just that – how can I explain it?"

"Try English."

"I came in my pants a minute ago."

"You what?"

"Came in my pants. I don't know if I can get hard again."

"Oh shit," she said.

"I'm sorry," said Jeffrey. "I really am."

"What did you come in your pants for?"

"I couldn't help it. No self-control."

"Ah. You're a virgin."

"What makes you think that?"

"You act like one – we all start out that way, no big thing."

"Okay, I'll admit it," he said.

"You're definitely not the only virgin at Princeton," she replied. "Hey, c'mon, I'm sure you can get in the mood again if you give yourself a chance. Why don't you just relax a little, okay? C'mon now, lie down ... you can relax here with me ... everything's safe and I like just really like being with you like this ... ah, that's better, get them off and enjoy my waterbed ... yeah, you can watch me ... ah, that's good ... real good ..."

It was the only solution – give him some sort of sexual hypnotic command. Jeffrey moved around on the bed which rolled and pitched like the incoming tide. In all of forty-five seconds he was raring to go, and he didn't collapse for two hours.

"I'll bet you didn't know your own strength," she said at last, lying blissfully spent beside him. "In fact you make Jonathan look like a puppy."

"You've – uh, done it with Jonathan?" said Jeffrey.

"Sure, we had a thing together for a while last spring. But he's so emotionally immature. You know how cowboys are – so scared by sex they can hardly get it up. They put on a big show, but when you get them in bed it's wham-bam thank-you-ma'am, and there they go, running back to their horse."

"What?"

"Besides, rumor has it that Bernie has the hots for Jonathan and so that's that."

"But – that's gross," Jeffrey blurted out.

"Get used to it, Jeffrey. Life's weird."

CIA Behavioral Tests May Have Cost Millions; Included Sex Pattern Control

From Times Wire Services

WASHINGTON—The CIA Tuesday released more top-secret documents showing that its mind and behavior control experiments had included attempts at "alteration of sex patterns" and drug tests on college students.

In responding to requests submitted under the Freedom of Information Act, the agency made available 415 heavily censored pages from a pile of documents on the experiments it had conducted on willing and unwitting Americans in the 1950s and '60s.

CIA Director Stansfield Turner said the documents on the controversial projects, already investigated by Senate committees on the basis of partial evidence, had been discovered recently in "retired archives filed under financial accounts."

Turner and a panel of former CIA experts in the behavior projects were to testify today at Senate hearings.

General outlines of the discontinued mind and behavior control projects—run under the codenames MK ULTRA, MK DELTA, Artichoke and Bluebird—had been disclosed in earlier investigations.

But the material released Tuesday gave the first indication of the scope and cost of the operation. It showed costs might have run into the tens of millions of dollars, with payments as large as $100,000 made to subcontracting institutions, hospitals, doctors, psychiatrists, hypnotists and others assigned to carry out the experiments.

The program, begun in the early cold war years as an effort to counteract alleged Soviet and Chinese brainwashing techniques, tapered off through the 1960s and was terminated in 1973.

The names of the institutions and individuals were blacked out in copies supplied to reporters. They were reported to include some prominent experts and prestigious hospitals—some, perhaps, had been unaware they were working in projects funded by CIA-controlled "front" organizations.

However, the New York Times reported Tuesday that the CIA had channeled funds through three private medical research foundations: the Geschickter Foundation for Medical Research of Washington, the Josiah Macy Jr. Foundation and the now-defunct Society for the Investigation of Human Ecology, Inc.

The director of the $50 million Macy Foundation, Dr. John W. Bowers, denied any link to the CIA. Dr. Charles F. Geschickter, a pathologist associated with Georgetown University, referred inquiries about the foundation that is registered in his name to a lawyer who represents the university.

The lawyer, Vincent Fuller, said there would be no comment until Georgetown had finished its investigation into any relationship it might have had with the CIA.

UNWITTING SUBJECT—Frank R. Olson killed himself after he was given LSD in a drink.

AP photo

Among other things in its article on the CIA, the New York Times said that:

—The Geschickter Foundation had given $3 million to the university for construction of a medical school building.

—The defunct foundation had funded experiments on isolation and sensory deprivation conducted by the late Dr. D. Ewen Cameron of the Allan Memorial Institute of Psychiatry at McGill University in Montreal.

—That foundation had also underwritten drug experiments on mental patients and staff members of the Butler Memorial Hospital in Providence, R.I.

—The same foundation, largely run by the CIA, had been given the appearance of being associated with the Cornell University Medical Center. It had been set up under the direction of Dr. Harold Wolff, a psychiatrist and an authority on pain, who sought to collect information about "brainwashing."

One uncensored name in the material released by the CIA was that of Dr. Sidney Gottlieb, former chief of the agency's chemical and scientific division, who ran MK ULTRA and similar projects for many years. He was last reported to have been in retirement abroad.

One "memorandum for the record," written by Gottlieb and dated June 9, 1953, said that "Dr. (censored) at his two facilities" was working on LSD "and related materials."

The New York Times reported that Dr. Carl Pfeiffer, a pharmacologist, had conducted LSD experiments for the CIA on prisoners at the federal penitentiary in Atlanta and the Bordentown Reformatory in New Jersey between 1955 and 1964. He is now associated with a private treatment center in New Jersey.

—The memorandum said emphasis would be placed on translating basic data "into operationally pertinent material" covering such areas as "alteration of sex patterns," "disturbance of memory" and "discrediting by aberrant behavior."

Gottlieb said the cost of the project "will not exceed $86,553 for the period from July 5, 1953 to July 4, 1954."

The documents did not indicate what had come of the experiments or what was meant by "alteration of sex patterns," but Gottlieb did say results would be put into "an operational field manual."

The earlier congressional investigations showed that drug and mind control experiments had been carried out on both volunteers and unwitting subjects, including servicemen, prisoners, and drug addicts.

One unwitting subject, an Army scientist, Frank R. Olson, committed suicide soon after receiving a drink laced with LSD at a CIA-sponsored reception.

Meanwhile, NBC News said in a television report that classified documents had been uncovered showing that the CIA's experiments on humans with drugs had been much more extensive than the CIA has admitted.

The network said the documents indicated that the drug experiments had not ended a decade ago, as the CIA and the Army Chemical Corps have stated, but "may have continued until recently."

11. Endless Void

There was a hill, the highest one near the Institute, where Jonathan liked to retreat sometimes. The climb to the top went through a woodsy region and a couple little meadows, past three abandoned weather-beaten roof-shot barns and several ramshackle fences with ant-conquered split logs, sudden sharp rock outcroppings and then this trickling clear-water stream.

He paused for a sip of water at a place where the brook flowed into a large silent pool. He'd read of water pollution even in these seemingly pristine creeks, but the water was sweet and reminded him of home and the creek behind the barn ... he'd spent a lot of his childhood along that stream. Coyote Creek it was called. Almost dry in summer, a calm autumn flow, a sometimes frozen brook in winter, a raging river in the spring. His chest felt that goddamn pang of homesickness. The last time he'd been home, for a week last summer, it had been horrible. His father had reached a point where he wouldn't even speak to him because he was so dead set against Jonathan continuing to work at the Institute. And now in a letter, his dad had just blamed Jonathan's decision not to go home for Christmas this year on the Institute and the hypnotic conditions.

The letter had arrived that very morning, accusing Jonathan of having no concern at all for the feelings of his dead mother and his brothers. His Dad had pointed out that it was the first Christmas ever that Jonathan hadn't spent at home – and that since Jonathan would probably be in the army next year, and might even be off fighting for his country in Vietnam by then, this was probably the last chance they'd have to spend Christmas as a family for a long time.

And then to top things off, his Dad had enclosed a copy of the confidential infirmary report that he had received from Dr. Dalrymple about the crazy episode last spring. Jonathan had the crumpled report in his pocket, where he'd crammed it instead of deep sixing it right away like he probably should have. Just for the hell of it, he took it out and read it again:

INFIRMARY REPORT

April 18, 1966
Student: Jonathan Selby Smith
Class: Junior
Admitted for: Extreme anxiety, paranoia

Dear Mr. Smith:

I feel obligated to inform you that your son, Jonathan, was admitted as an in-patient for two days of psychological and medical testing at the Princeton Infirmary, following a period of withdrawal and paranoia.

Jonathan was experiencing extreme generalized anxiety and fear that he was in danger from some unspecified threat. The closest he came to describing it was to say that it was as though 'the Bogeyman' was out to get him.

I discovered that Jonathan was suffering from noticeable memory loss. Some of his symptoms were of a hallucinatory nature. For example, he said he had a vague feeling that the metal objects in the room were going to rust and deteriorate soon. He also expressed the delusional ideation that he could leave his body anytime he wanted, and that he could even become a dove.

He informed me that he has been a long-term voluntary subject in a series of experiments involving deep hypnosis, which are designed to alter one's sense of reality. These experiments have been taking place at the New Jersey Neuro-Psychiatric Institute.

Jonathan is not the first student-subject in the experiments to seek help at the Princeton Infirmary. We have seen several other cases where formerly well-adjusted students came to us experiencing intense psychological traumas and disorientation. We have also seen other memory-loss problems.

I advised Jonathan that, given his present state of mind, it would not be prudent for him to continue to allow himself to be subjected to hypnosis, not even infrequently. However, I encountered considerable resistance to any suggestion on my part that he disaffiliate himself from those experiments and seek private psychotherapy.

Though the paranoia incident abated, and Jonathan apparently was functioning satisfactorily upon the completion of our psychological tests, my main concern at this point is that his memory loss could recur, or that if he insists on continuing the hypnotic experimentation, there possibly could be long-term memory impairment and disorientation.

Dr. Willard Dalrymple, M.D.
Princeton Infirmary

Jonathan put away the infirmary report and continued climbing toward the top of the hill. There was his dad, sounding half-crazy from the Princeton perspective. And there was Bernie, his lips, his weirdness – and there was Pok whom he felt was like a brother in heart, in spirit, in life. And then there was Anne. What a strong pull he felt toward her. It was physical attraction, but it was more. He'd wanted to have a continuing relationship with the same girl ever since he could remember, somebody who loved him. He had to laugh to himself when he realized he wanted the love to be sort of like his dog had loved him, unconditional love – that was the love-heart involvement he'd begun seeking after his mom had died.

As he got to the top of the hill he was slightly out of breath, even though he'd been staying in shape with fencing. He sat down cross-legged, a Princeton Indian in cowboy boots that hurt his left heel like crazy – gotta get them fixed, he resolved to himself.

A cool breeze moving his way brought a languid rush of all the scents commingling out there in the woods and the stream with its moldy leaves and sparkling splashes of tiny waterfalls times a hundred thousand – he inhaled, the air tickling his nostrils and almost making him sneeze. And then something happened that jolted him but also suddenly made him feel vastly better.

He experienced a pop in his head and suddenly he was somehow just totally present where he was sitting passively breathing the air and taking in all the sounds around him in the meadow, in the forest, in the trees, in the air – even in the ground, he thought to himself, if he put his ear down and really listened.

He found himself looking down thirty feet away where there was movement in the woods. A doe and her half-grown fawn were emerging into a small clear space. The fawn gamboled ahead of its mother. The doe paused at the edge of the clearing. She raised her head to listen, her large sensitive ears forward attentively, her concentration focused entirely on her perceptual world – just like a Zen master, Jonathan thought.

The doe slowly turned her head and looked directly at Jonathan. She sniffed the air with flared nostrils, trying to pick up his scent. They stared at each other. Jonathan suddenly remembered the one deer he had killed. He had gone out with his first .22 single-shot rifle when he was a ten year old, playing out the Daniel Boone myth of being the great hunter. A young buck had suddenly appeared, and Jonathan had automatically raised his rifle, sighted down the barrel, and pulled the trigger.

The buck had remained frozen after the sound of the discharge of the rifle had forever cracked the silence. Then the animal had slowly crumpled, its life-force blasted away. Jonathan had walked, stunned, over to the deer. A small hole had been made where the bullet had entered its head; a gaping hole showed where the bullet had left the other side of the skull. Jonathan had stared in total disbelief as a wave of psychic shock had fried his nervous system. Then he had thrown his rifle down hard onto the ground and had run away crying.

The weather took a sudden change. Wind picked up and storm clouds rolled fast overhead. Jonathan gave up his solitary meadow and its mixed emotional inputs, made his way back to his MG and put up the top. As it started to drizzle and then downpour, Jonathan drove uncharacteristically slowly through the rain, watching with full attention the windshield wipers rhythmically wiping away the small circles of rain that pounded the glass. It was soothing, the coming and going of the raindrops. He wished he could drive on forever.

But then there he was, already at the driveway to the Institute for yet another session with Jeffrey. He drove off the driveway and stopped just ten feet from the lake, which was being pounded, albeit very gently, by literally billions of tiny drops that Jonathan was taking in as a visual whole, a gust of wind suddenly rushing across the surface of the lake, altering the blue-gray hues suddenly from light to quite dark. 'Ruach,' Jonathan thought, remembering from Sunday school the Hebrew word for the breath of God. In a few more days or weeks the lake would be frozen again, God's life-giving wet breath turning to snow. Jonathan liked the change from liquid to solid, when the first snowfall transformed the universe into pure virgin hopeful white. Just that last winter, Jonathan was now remembering out of the blue, Bernie had taken him for walks on the iced-over lake at the Institute. What was that memory? It had been something about being made of ice. Yes, that was the condition – 'Jonathan, when you wake up you will feel that you are ice, the same as the lake outside.' Bernie had stepped out onto the ice with him and had told Jonathan to lie down on the solid surface and feel completely at one with it. But when Bernie had taken him back inside, Jonathan now remembered how he had freaked out, totally panicked that he was going to melt. It had been such a frightening feeling! Bernie had strengthened the trance and told him not to be afraid, to go ahead and melt, to enjoy the feeling of turning from a solid into a liquid ...

That had been one hell of a condition, thought Jonathan as he drove up the long Institute driveway through the rain. But wait – why was he starting to remember those conditions, when he was under a post-hypnotic condition not to remember?

He exhaled with a loud rushing pulse of air – he didn't care why anything was happening. Something inside made him want to remember – remember! This was a life or death situation ... but even now, that memory was fading again – everything was now fading away into the loud patter of rain on his canvas top as he drove into the Institute parking lot, killed the engine and hurried out of the chill of the rain.

Upon entering the Institute, it was almost habitual that Jonathan went first into the kitchen for some seriously-needed coffee. Jeffrey was already there, hanging out like an old pro with Bernie, Mike, Linda and two other subjects. Jonathan wanted to check with Bernie on how his draft deferment looked for the next year, but he could see that Bernie was into one of his off-center hocus-pocus mumbo-jumbo trips, talking with gregarious enthusiasm about the trail-blazing Zen implications of the Institute's revolutionary hypnosis research.

Jonathan noticed that Bernie was turning his most enthusiastic vibes toward Jeffrey, who was rising to the bait like an adolescent trout to a colorful fake fly. Having heard the same Institute party line about consciousness-expansion about a hundred times before, Jonathan told Jeffrey he'd meet him downstairs when Jeffrey was ready, took his cup of coffee and made his escape.

He went down the basement hall to his hypnosis room. Even after he lit some incense and a candle and sat down and did some deep breathing exercises, he still felt out of harmony, bummed out about life in general. Last year and the year before, it had always been Pok who'd helped him up when he felt down. Pok would remind him that after all, the whole world was nothing more than a miniscule speck of dust spinning through an infinite endless void – so what was the sense of taking life so seriously? But even though what Pok had said was basically true, recently Jonathan couldn't help but take life seriously.

Suddenly Jeffrey walked in.

"Guess what?" he said, his loud excited voice disturbing the tranquility of the room. "Bernie just told me that I can be a subject once a week in the EEG experiments."

"Are you sure you want to get into that?" said Jonathan.

"Sure I'm sure. Bernie said it won't interfere with our hypnosis work at all. It sounds fantastic. He says that in less than six weeks I'll be able to control my alpha state completely at will, so that whenever I want to, no matter what's going on, I will be able just to close my eyes and go right into a meditative alpha state – just like that!" He snapped his fingers. "Have you been trained to do that yet?"

"Uhm, I gave it a try last year, but I decided that meditation wasn't the kind of thing I wanted to have programmed into me like I was one of Pavlov's dogs or something."

"But Bernie says that you can achieve the same alpha states in six weeks using his equipment that it takes Zen Masters twenty years to attain."

"Well, Jeffrey, as far as I'm concerned, you can interpret those results any way you want. Mike has logged about a hundred hours on that instant satori machine, and he's hardly what you'd call an enlightened Bodhisattva."

"What's a Bodhisattva?"

"Well, in the Mahayana and Ch'in Buddhist traditions, a Bodhisattva is a person who attains total enlightenment, who transcends the material human sphere altogether. A Bodhisattva is free of all mortal karmic restrictions but he chooses, through his infinite love and compassion, to return to the earth and work for the spiritual advancement of humankind. Or something like that."

"Wow."

Twenty minutes later Jeffrey was once again in a deep hypnotic trance. There, Jonathan said to himself. Got him all the way down. Breathing regular and deep. No signs of any eye movement – definitely stage-four sleep. What to do? Tell him that when he wakes up, he'll be a toad? Or give him a condition to wake up into the great blank void? Wake him up as a Bodhisattva? Or the Bogeyman?

An image came to Jonathan's mind of Jeffrey heading through the hypnotic conditions like a calf headed down the long wooden chute back home at the cutting corrals. The calf could look ahead and see light at the end of the chute and he'd assume that as soon as he hit the light he'd be in the clear again – but the celestial joke was that at the end of the long dark chute, right where the light opened up, the chute would squeeze tight with three men on the metal levers, ready to slam the gates shut both behind and in front of the calf.

Back home the youngster calf was branded, earmarked and then rolled onto his side and castrated. Here at the Institute it was a little different. Jeffrey was running down the hypnosis chute with his eyes on the great light ahead, expecting hypnosis to magically enlighten him. But as soon as he started with the actual test conditions, the guiding light could go out at any moment.

Jonathan looked intensely at Jeffrey. This was his very own subject, hypnotized and open to experiencing anything that Jonathan cared to suggest to his unconscious. This was exactly how the Institute had also kept Jonathan on a psychological choke-leash, for way over a year.

But wait – what am I supposed to be doing here, Jonathan said to himself, pulling his mind back to the work at hand. What condition today should he use as an exercise for Jeffrey? Well, there was the condition Bernie had given – yes, he was remembering it now – strange, the way the conditions were creeping back into his memory, refusing to cooperate with Bernie's past commands. This one was the condition when Jonathan had awakened and felt as though he were six inches tall – a classic schizophrenic perceptual distortion, and Jonathan had freaked out as predicted. But ... sometimes he still became momentarily panicked that somebody was going to step on him. So aha, that was where that anxiety came from! Bernie must not have completely erased it – or maybe erasing a condition sometimes simply didn't work. Whatever – that six-inch experience was definitely nothing Jonathan wanted to lay on Jeffrey.

Oh yeah, and there had been that condition to be weightless, entirely free of gravity – but this time in his own body, not inside the body of a dove. As a result of the condition, Jonathan's perception of weight had been radically distorted, his brain apparently feeding him entirely contradictory sensory read-outs compared to what his body knew to be the truth.

Jonathan was astonished that it was all coming back to mind. Like, walking with Bernie under some condition, going outside, walking up the hill behind the Institute and suddenly not being able to tell up from down, completely losing his sense of balance ... and then falling, falling up, then down, then suddenly sideways and oh God, falling down, down and then smashing into a giant rock and going entirely out, unconscious . . . . and then waking up in Bernie's office in a reclining chair with blood dripping from his forehead and Bernie telling him that everything was okay, that he'd just taken a little fall and that was all –

Sitting there in the little hypnosis cubicle with his subject in a trance awaiting an exciting new condition, Jonathan gasped for air. He was literally shaking right down into the core of his psyche. Goddamnit, Bernie!–he thought – you never removed that condition!

Jonathan stood up on numb legs. He knew he had to see Bernie right away, before he forgot the whole thing again and everything was again lost – just like that time he'd flown out the window as a dove and a part of him had never come back.

"Okay, I want you just to relax, Jeffrey," his voice was saying on automatic, "just sleep calmly until I return in a little while. Just sleep, that's good – sleep."

He closed the door behind him and hurried upstairs.

"Jonathan, I really need to talk to you," said Linda in a very serious voice.

He didn't pay any attention to her, he went right on up the stairs – oh shit, suddenly he was feeling as if he were falling over backwards, that weightless, floating, disoriented feeling hitting him again as he climbed. He got to the top and walked on wobbly boots down the corridor and banged in unannounced into Bernie's inner office.

"Bernie, I've got to talk to you."

Bernie was in an afternoon conference with Mike but motioned for Mike to leave. "Of course, Jonathan, what's the matter, sit down."

"I don't want to sit down."

"Where's Jeffrey?"

"He's okay. But I just remembered that you never removed that condition, goddamnit, you left me in that condition and I've been walking around for six months like a chicken with its head cut off, goddamnit, you forgot to–"

"Now relax, Jonathan. What condition?"

Jonathan was shaking so much he could hardly talk. "That time when I fell, that time when you made me weightless and I lost my balance and fell down the hill – you never removed that condition, I'm still under that condition!"

"Jonathan, please, relax. Of course I removed that condition. I'd never forget something as important as that. You know I wouldn't."

"Well, I don't remember you removing it, goddamnit!"

"Of course, you received a post-hypnotic condition not to remember any of it. Sit down, Jonathan. There in the reclining chair."

"I don't want to."

"Jonathan, if you don't do as I say, you're going to remain in that frightened place you're in forever. You've got to let me help you."

Jonathan held his ground.

"Sit down, Jonathan."

Jonathan gave one last inner effort to retain his own will against those eyes, but it was too much for him. His energy was depleted. He sat down.

"Good. Thank you. Now just relax and listen to my voice. Everything's going to be okay, you've just had a little upset. Relax, feel the secure sensation of being within the realm of my protective love and power. Nothing can touch you, I'll take care of everything. You did the right thing in coming to me just now. You trust me and now I'm going to help you. We're going to push ahead to where you won't ever have to worry about this kind of problem again. Just go ahead and take a deep breath."

Jonathan tried to find something inside to grab onto, some rung of the hypnosis ladder that would keep him from slipping down, down, down as Bernie started talking him into a trance. He struggled to remain conscious by trying to bring Anne's face to mind but Bernie's voice was so pervasive that Jonathan's focus of awareness was slipping, slipping ... into a quiet, soft, warm, womb-like ..."Callubra-callorum."

Falling, falling, down, down ...

"You are now going deeper and deeper into trance, enjoying the feeling of total relaxation and submission which you have experienced so many times before. You are slowly losing consciousness as I lower you deeper and deeper into the dark peaceful hypnotic well of sleep and relaxation."

Jonathan struggled with all his strength to remain conscious and not go under but he was losing ground, his grip was slipping with every word Bernie said, until finally he reached the point where he knew he had lost again ...

There was an acute spell of silence. After what seemed like years of waiting, he heard Bernie's voice.

"Now, Jonathan, you are completely hypnotized and as always, what I tell you now will remain with you until I retract the condition. The condition of weightlessness, which you believe I forgot to remove after your fall, is now completely erased. Any residue effects are now completely gone. Is that clear?"

Jonathan's head was motionless a moment, then nodded.

"When you wake up, you won't remember what has happened today regarding the condition of weightlessness. Do you understand?"

"Yes."

"Good. Now you are leaving the deep well, you are on a raft on a calm sea, slowly rocking back and forth. Do you feel the raft under you?"

"Uhm, yeah."

"Concentrate on the raft, the rhythm of the rocking, back and forth, back and forth. And keep listening to my voice. You must trust me, Jonathan. Last year, when you were working through your relationship with your dad, you resisted me at first. Do you remember?"

"Yes."

"But I persevered and you finally gave in. You were honest with me and I helped you. Is that right?"

"Right."

"And now it's time for you to be as honest about this new relationship with this girl Anne, as you were about your relationship with your father. We can't have anything interfering with your progress."

Jonathan felt dizzy. Nauseous.

"Listen to me, Jonathan. Listen to my voice. If you're going to work at this Institute you've got to be very careful what kind of people you allow yourself to get involved with. You wouldn't want anything to interfere with our work together, would you?"

"No."

"So you've got to struggle to overcome your weaknesses, just as I do, and Mike does and just as Jeffrey must if he's going to continue working here. Now I want you to tell me what's been going on between you and that girl."

Silence.

Bernie began talking again.

"When did you last see her?"

"Last weekend."

"All right, you are now gradually floating off on the raft ... moving through the gentle sea, going back in time ... it's a few days ago ... last weekend. You're with Anne. Can you tell me where you are?"

"In my room."

"Is she with you?"

"Yes."

"How do you feel?"

Jonathan was entirely there again, in his room with Anne. "I feel horny."

"Tell me about it."

"I'm just uptight. I don't know what's going to happen next."

"Do you touch her?"

"Yeah."

"Does she touch you?"

"Yeah."

"And you feel frightened?"

"No. Yes."

"Which is it? No or yes?"

"Yes. A little."

"It's that she's too close, isn't it? A woman has come too close to you again, just like the other times. Is that why you feel a little frightened?"

"Maybe. Yeah."

"Is it a suffocating feeling?"

"No."

"No?"

"Well, yeah. Maybe a little."

"You're afraid of losing your freedom to a woman. Is that it?"

"I don't know."

"You're being defensive, Jonathan. Yes or no?"

"Maybe so."

"Then the answer is yes."

"Yes. But maybe I want it."

"Want to lose your freedom to a woman?"

"Yes."

"Is it because you're feeling weak?"

Silence.

"I said, is it because you're feeling too weak to stand on your own?"

"I like feeling weak sometimes. With her."

"But you agreed to overcome that feeling, didn't you, Jonathan? You told me you feel strongest when you're alone, when you're not involved in a romantic relationship that affects your judgment. Have you told Anne all about your work here?"

"Yes."

"Didn't I tell you not to discuss the work with anyone outside the Institute?"

"But I needed to talk about it."

"What did Anne say about our work?"

"She doesn't like it. She says I should stop."

Silence a moment.

"Well then – I want you to go very deep now, Jonathan, deep down into the welcoming well."

Jonathan reached out for the side of the well, thinking of Anne, holding onto the image of her smiling loving face. He had to remember. He had to fight ...

"Now you can see that the soft forgetful fog is floating down into the well and covering up my words so that you won't remember anything at all that's happened in this session. You won't remember anything about your fear of having been in the weightless condition, which is now erased. And you won't remember we've talked about Anne. And here is a new condition for you: Your fear of having a close relationship with Anne will increase. The next time you're close to her you'll feel suffocated, bothered – you'll feel unfriendly toward her. You will decide to cut off all contact with her. Avoid her entirely, Jonathan. Then you'll feel strong and beautifully centered again. Do you understand?"

"Yes."

"Now my words, and all memories of this session, are being swallowed by the great white fog. The fog is pouring down into your well, surrounding you. It's thick and white, you can't see through it. It covers all my words. And now the only way out of the fog is to let go and wake up. And when you wake up, you won't remember this condition. You'll feel refreshed, and the upset you experienced earlier will be gone ... so just relax ... breathe ... let go of the memories ..."

12. Cowboys Never Cry

Pok had two tickets for the Maharishi Mahesh Yogi's talk in New York. Jonathan instantly accepted the offer to cut fencing practice and head for Madison Square Garden to find out what the guru of the Beatles would have to say to thousands of college kids who were all in quest of the secret of satori – the ultimate state of inner peace.

Pok and Jonathan took the bus rather than fight traffic in the MG. The Port Authority Terminal was a zoo to say the least. More army uniforms than Gandhi could shake a stick at – young guys about Jonathan's and Pok's age with their hair cut right down to the scalp, just out of boot camp with one-way tickets to Vietnam in their pockets. Vacant stares galore. "Whoopee we're all gonna die," said Pok, walking along saluting every man in uniform he passed.

"Hey, you're going to taunt one of those guys into pounding on your psychedelic noggin if you're not careful," Jonathan warned him.

"I'm just practicing saluting, seeing how it feels. Sort of fun playing soldier boy."

"You've got to be kidding."

"Come on, Jonathan, loosen up. What's the problem, amigo?"

"I don't know, maybe it's my turn to crash. What happened to bring your mood up – letter from Shana?"

"No chance of that. It's just hard to keep a top dog down, I was bound to resurface sometime."

"Well let's hope it lasts. Hold on a minute, I want to make a phone call."

"To who, your draft board?"

"Anne."

"Hey, tickets were sold out for the Maharishi a week ago, you're not going to be able to sneak her in and you know it."

"I guess you're right," said Jonathan, but he dropped a coin into the nearest pay phone anyway. "I need to talk with her, I've got something to tell her and I want to get it off my mind."

"Well hurry up or we'll be late for the Enlightened One."

"Right."

Jonathan dialed the number he knew by heart, which was pounding loud as the phone rang. He could see her face, her doe's eyes looking at him softly – and he hung up the phone before she could answer.

"No one there?" Pok asked.

"I think I dialed the wrong number."

"You look like you just saw the Bogeyman. You all right?"

Jonathan was shaking, totally nervous for no reason at all. Anne was upsetting his whole world and he was ready to finish the relationship once and for all, get free of all the anxiety and stress she was causing him. One short phone call, the coup de grace, and that would be it, no more Anne. He dialed her number again, determined to be strong, trying not to succumb to the feelings of weakness she sometimes brought out in him.

"Hello?"

"Uhm, this is Jonathan."

"Hi, I was hoping you'd call."

"Listen, I've got something to tell you."

"What's that?"

He glanced at Pok, who was eavesdropping a few feet away. "Well ..." He felt unable to talk to her in such a public place.

"Listen, I'm in New York, at the bus terminal. What if I come over, are you busy?"

"No, just finishing a painting. You're in New York?"

"Right. I'll drop by in fifteen, twenty minutes, whatever it takes by taxi."

"I'll put on some tea. Are you hungry?"

"Uhm, no. See you then."

He hung up, shaking in his cowboy boots.

"Now just what the hell was that all about, telling her you'd come over?" Pok asked. "You're going to miss the words of the Holy One."

"Here," said Jonathan, "give some soldier my ticket, it'll help him more than me."

"Some friend. I had a dozen guys wanting to come with me, and I give my one extra ticket to you and you treat it like a paper airplane, fold it up and fly it on its way to some soldier boy. Thanks for everything puchito." He stomped away.

Jonathan stood staring at him until Pok disappeared into the crowd. Jonathan felt an impulse to go running after him – but instead he went to stand by a curb and hail a cab.

As soon as Jonathan buzzed the doorbell, Anne opened the door to her Village flat. She was wearing a simple white dress with tanned arms and legs showing. She greeted him by holding him close for a long moment and kissing him. When she sensed that he wasn't responsive, she slowly backed away to look up into his eyes.

"Long day," he said as an excuse for his coldness, and he walked into the living room and took off his boots in deference to her roommate's expensive rugs – then collapsed onto the sofa.

"Tea?" she said.

"Uhm, yeah, sure. No, what about a beer or some wine – anything like that around?"

"Well, actually, I don't think so."

"Hmm. Then some coffee."

"Neither of us drinks coffee. I told you we were seeing what life is like without drugs for a month, remember?"

"Hey, since when is coffee a drug, I mean really," he said. "And if coffee is a drug, then tea is, too. Anyway, I won't drink anything. I'm not thirsty."

"Jonathan, what's wrong?"

"Nothing."

He was growing even more inward and withdrawn, she could feel it. She sat down on an easy chair across from him rather than join him on the sofa where they'd made love just a week ago. There was more silence. Cars made obscene noises outside. Jonathan stared at his hands, then at the complex design of the Persian rug.

"You've gone away," she said.

There was a sensation of falling, falling away endlessly. It crept up on him suddenly, without warning. He felt dizzy. Bewildered. 'Go ahead and fall, Jonathan,' said Bernie's voice, 'Fall until I catch you –'

"I was just thinking," he said finally, not looking at her.

"What about?"

"Something from hypnosis. Something I'm not supposed to remember."

"What was it?"

"I don't know. It was something about you – something Bernie told me about you. Jesus, I wish I could remember!"

Jonathan felt even weaker inside, he had to put all his strength into trying just to keep his cool and hold his emotions in check so they wouldn't explode out into the open.

"So – are you feeling depressed?"

"I don't know."

"Are you angry?"

"I don't know. Stop asking me all these questions about how I feel!"

"You don't have to yell," she said. "I'm just trying to help."

"Why should you want to help?"

"Because I care about you."

"I don't see why anybody should care about me."

"Why not?"

He felt that suffocating feeling coming over him. "Goddamn, I can hardly breathe."

"Why can't you breathe?"

"I don't know. I just can't."

Anne looked steadily at him until he finally raised his eyes. When he found her looking right into his eyes something definitely made him angry. "What are you trying to do, hypnotize me with that stare of yours?" he fired at her.

His words hit her so hard that she couldn't hold back tears.

"Oh Jesus Christ, what's the matter now?"

She didn't say anything.

"Listen," he finally said, "I'm just overworked and ready to blow a fuse, that's all. I've got this senior thesis to get done and they're hassling me at the Psych Department, they don't want Bernie as my official advisor on the project, even though I came up with the idea with his help. And even though I'm almost done, they're still dead-set against the whole theme of the experiment."

"You mean your idea about testing LSD users at Princeton with EEG equipment?"

"Right – to see if their brainwaves are in fact changed after taking four or more trips on acid. Bernie somehow got me a grant to do it – a pile of money, forty-six grand to be precise.

People somewhere want the research done but Princeton is furious because I want to use students as subjects for the study. They can't take it – especially after the fallout in the press from that questionnaire study I did. I told you about that?"

"Yes."

"Well anyway I've got that project on my back, and Coach on my back, and Bernie on my back, and my work as a hypnotist on my back, and I just don't need any more hassles in my life, that's all I'm trying to say."

"And you think I'm just another hassle?"

He was inspecting a bruised fingernail on his left hand, his fencing hand, where he'd gotten banged up during practice. "I don't know. I'm just feeling like I need some space in my life or I'll go crazy."

"You want to back away from me, is that what you're trying to say?" Anne asked him with a sensitive, penetrating gaze.

"I don't know."

"Say what you mean, Jonathan. You're not being fair to me if you don't –"

He fired her a glance. "There you go, putting pressure on me all the time, that's what I'm talking about, here I am trying to hold my world together at Princeton and the Institute, and I've got this broad in New York always on my back – and I tell you, I'm just about ready to blow!"

Anne stood up. "Well, you listen to me – I've bent over backwards to understand you and to accept you just the way you are, even though it's obvious that you've let yourself get totally messed up with hypnosis and drugs. But I'm not going to lie down and take shit from you. I'm not just some broad in New York, and you'd better know it right now. Either stop attacking me or get out of my apartment."

Jonathan just stared at her in amazement. Deep down inside he felt tears welling up, threatening his entire image. Cowboys don't cry, that was one hard lesson he had learned early in life. But right at that moment he could feel the old choking in the throat, the burning in his eyes, the tensions in his chest ready to burst into sobs – and before he completely blew his cool, he put his boots back on and went stomping toward her door, shouting at her that she was just like all the rest of the women he'd ever known and he was tired of being led around by the balls.

"So if that's the way you're going to be with me, fuck you," he shouted, slamming the door behind him as he headed out down the hall.

Abandoned Bureau of Research,
New Jersey Neuro-Psychiatric Institute

U.S.NEWS

JANUARY 24, 1994 & WORLD REPORT $2.50

COLD WAR GUINEA PIGS

The government's secret experiments using radiation, mind control, chemicals and drugs on its citizens

13. Forces of Darkness Strike Again

Jeffrey went up the long stairwell, uncertain of whether he was even in the right entry of Little Hall. He felt jittery to be in upper class territory. His boots made a racket on the stone steps and by the time he made it to the very top, by the door to Jonathan's attic room, he was panting like a dog.

Jonathan had told him to feel free to stop by anytime. Now this was the moment of truth, time to knock on the door, and he was losing his nerve. What if Jonathan was in there with some wild hippie girl? Or even half a dozen wild hippie girls? Or worse still, what if Jonathan was experimenting with some new psychedelic and was in a weird state of mind? Jeffrey thought about turning around and running back down the stairs. He should have phoned ahead instead of just coming over.

But instead of running, Jeffrey remembered how Jonathan had taught him to watch his breathing whenever he felt really anxious. Inhale, exhale. Feel your head in the sky and your feet on the ground. Relax and let the good times roll ... he gave three soft confident raps on the old door.

He could hear music coming from inside. After a few moments without an answer, he decided that the music was too loud for anyone to have heard him, so he raised his hand to try again, louder.

Just before his knuckles struck wood, he heard a voice from inside. "What's that?"

"Uhm, this is Jeffrey, is that you, Jonathan?"

"He's not here. What do you want?"

"Uhm, Jonathan's my hypnotist, out at the New Jersey Neuro-Psychiatric Institute. I was just stopping by to –"

"Hold on," said the voice, and Jeffrey heard the sound of a bolt lock being snapped. Then the door opened.

His first impression of the person he found facing him was of a young man who had just returned from a trip around the world – in a box car. The guy was wearing trousers that must have been among the first ten pairs that Levi ever made. And his tee shirt had enough holes in it to strain spaghetti. He also had a very definite but pleasant odor – almost like a perfume.

"So you're the famous first subject," the guy said, with a curious grin that seemed to keep expanding. "Jonathan's been telling me about you. Come on in. From one zombie to another, glad to meet you. I'm Pok."

"Hi, Pok. Pleased to meet you."

Jeffrey automatically offered his hand to shake, and Pok slapped his hand instead. "Gimme five, brother," said Pok. Jeffrey cautiously walked inside. "Hey, where'd you get those duds?" Pok continued. "You look just like Roy Rogers on his way back from the stables."

"Roy Rogers? You've got to be kidding, this is clothes like Bob Dylan wears. Jonathan even agrees."

"We're all entitled to our pet fantasies, Roy." Pok sat down on a decorative pillow in the middle of the room. "If you want to be Bob Dylan, be Bob Dylan. Come on in, sit down, a friend of Jonathan's is a friend of mine as they say. I was just checking out some smuggled reading contraband that I found on Jonathan's desk, about the Institute. Sit, sit."

Jeffrey sat down on a decorative pillow too.

Jonathan's dorm room looked like a picture Jeffrey had seen in Playboy of the ideal hippie pad in San Francisco. He couldn't get over the big painting of the puckered, heavily lip-sticked lips.

"I haven't seen Jonathan since a few days ago at the Institute," Jeffrey replied. "I was hoping he'd be here."

"No such luck, it doesn't look like he came back from New York last night. We went to see the great almighty hot-wind guru – the Maharishi."

"Wow, were you there? I read about his Transcendental Meditation lecture in the New York Times this morning. It must have been groovy to be there in person." 'Groovy' was a new word in Jeffrey's budding hip vocabulary, right up there with 'karma,' 'uptight,' 'laid-back,' 'far out,' 'outa sight' and 'that's heavy.'

"Groovy was just the word for it," Pok said. "One hundred percent groovy hype. Total show, you didn't miss a thing. So how are you liking the zombie scene out at the Institute?"

"I wouldn't call it a zombie scene. I mean, it's really an amazing place. Jonathan said you were a subject there last year, right?"

Pok shrugged his shoulders, his expression clouding. Instead of responding, he picked up a stapled report and silently started reading it while Jeffrey soaked in the groovy atmosphere of Jonathan's room. There was a wide bed that certainly looked like it had seen some heavy action. And the room was littered with bunches of overgrown madras pillows everywhere. The narrow tall window had a view of the tops of other dorms that looked just like castles in the countryside of Europe. Not that Jeffrey had ever seen Europe, but he hoped to go some day. In fact, he planned to apply for the Princeton Summer Work Abroad program and hoped to go to France. His French was getting to be proficient enough that he figured he could probably qualify. The only question was whether his parents would agree. They might think it would be too expensive to fly to

France, even if he did have a job over in Paris, which he had constant dreams of getting to see – but his dreams wouldn't count for much. His parents were very practical people and the practical thing, of course, would be to live at home for the summer and get a job just a few miles away.

For some reason, the décor of Jonathan's room stimulated Jeffrey's fantasies and made him think of things like flying to Paris or working for a studio in Los Angeles. This room was actually a very psychologically stimulating environment to sit inside, thought Jeffrey. When Jonathan graduated, maybe Jonathan could fix things so that Jeffrey could move into this room, and that would be outa sight. Of course, Jeffrey's mother would probably never climb up all those stairs to inspect his new residence, but that would be okay with him. Finally he'd have his own place that wasn't certified with Mom's wax seal of approval.

"Jesus, listen to this," Pok said. "'Last year the funding for the New Jersey Neuro-Psychiatric Institute Bureau of Research was listed at six hundred thousand smackeroos – that's big bucks they have to kick around and that's not all. Get this – and I quote – 'The Institute's Bureau of Research in Neurology is supported financially by the State of New Jersey through funds appropriated under the Division of Mental Health and Hospitals, Department of Institutions and Agencies, and Grant Funds from the U.S. Public Health Service, National Science Foundation, private foundations, industry and private individuals.' That's one hell of a lot of loose money coming in to finance a loony-bin if you ask me."

"What do you mean?" Jeffrey asked, entirely confused.

"I mean this, Roy – when I was working out there I definitely got the impression that the Big Boys at the place were wearing a lot of different hats, if you catch my drift."

"My name's not Roy, it's Jeffrey – and I don't understand what you're implying."

"Listen to this from the report of last year's financing for the Institute. In 1966 there's a listing of funding from 'Other Sources' making a grand total of twenty-four thousand dollars. But now for 1967, that figure more than doubled – to fifty-two thousand dollars. Now just who do you suppose they're referring to when they talk about 'Other' sources of income?"

"I don't know – who do you think?"

"I think that the FBI or the CIA or somebody like that has their finger on the whole gang that's running that place, that's what I think."

"But why would the CIA want to –"

"Mind if I smoke?" Pok asked, cutting Jeffrey off in mid-sentence.

"No, of course not," said Jeffrey, noticing the handmade cigarette that Pok had just slipped from his shirt pocket.

"Damn, the forces of darkness have struck again, could I bother you for a match? I've run temporarily dry."

"There's some matches on the bookcase, I'll get them."

"Atta boy."

Fire flamed, Pok puffed, smoke curled up into the room. "Ahhh! Long live Ho Chi Minh," said Pok. "You want a hit?"

"Uhm, Jeez, is that marijuana?" Jeffrey asked nervously.

"I don't suppose you're a narc, are you?"

Jeffrey laughed, feeling himself trembling with excitement. Ever since reading in Playboy about marijuana, he'd been wanting to experience its effects. "I'd really like to try it, if you think it's safe."

Pok nailed him suddenly with a sober stare. "You find something that's safe and I'll show you something that's boring, amigo. Just being alive is totally unsafe. It's going to kill you in the end, right? As far as the Holy Herb goes, it sure as hell keeps the spirit brighter than almost anything else I've tried. And this is a special recipe from an old departed friend of mine. I call it Shana's Delight number 406. One half Acapulco gold, one half Panama red, and one half Afghani hash."

"Uhm, that makes one and a half."

"Exactly. What we've got here is a one hundred fifty percent high. Here, take a toke. You hold it like this, comrade. Put it to the lips and inhale, taking in a little air from outside along with the smoke, a little carburation to cool the toke and all that."

Jeffrey tried, but ended up coughing.

"Here, let me show you again, don't Bogart that joint, it goes like this –" Pok tilted his head back and inhaled with a sucking sound. "Ah yes indeed," he said, grinning. "The royal Incan cure for constipation of the giggles. Go for it!"

Jeffrey tried again and burned the skin right off his tonsils, but he held the smoke in, following Pok's recommendation. When he finally blew the air out, lots of smoke came out too.

"Is smoking marijuana anything like getting hypnotized?" he asked Pok, who was back to reading the reports on Jonathan's desk.

Pok looked up, as if startled out of some profound thought. He stared at Jeffrey for a moment as if he didn't recognize him at all. "Ah, it's you, Roy Rogers – hey, you wouldn't believe the shit in this report, I wonder how Jonathan got hold of it, it looks confidential to me, but get a load of this – 'Our studies in massage involve consideration of changes in self-concept, in attitudes toward others, in body image and tension levels. The role of massage in enhancing personal relationships is also being investigated.' That's just pure bullshit cover-up talk for what they're really doing out there. This whole report is nothing but hype to give a legal image to their research. I should know, they took me and held me under for the count."

"You mean ... uhm ... with hypnosis?"

"You look a little woozy there, Roy, what's going on inside that cabeza of yours? Take another toke, we gotta get your rocket off the ground."

"Thanks. I hope I don't cough this time. I haven't had much experience smoking. You know, I've only smoked cigarettes once."

"No kidding."

"It was a Marlboro."

"What was?"

"The cigarette I smoked half of."

"Half?"

"I threw it away in the middle," said Jeffrey. "I'm not too hot to get cancer, if you know what I mean."

"Hey, nobody is, kid. The big 'C' is no way to die. But this is the opposite of cancer."

Jeffrey tried again. There was a tickle in his throat but no cough this time. "Uhm," he said a long moment later, "I feel sort of – well, as if little people are running around inside my stomach. Is that normal?"

Pok grinned. "Totally normal." Then his expression shifted like lightning and he seemed to be feeling a pain. The hand that wasn't holding the joint slapped his left breast, then slapped his left pocket, and then went inside the pocket of his Levi's and came out with a piece of paper. He looked at it a moment while Jeffrey watched him. The little people inside Jeffrey's stomach had turned into a herd of rampaging elephants.

"Want to see a picture of a dead friend of mine?" Pok asked.

"What?" Jeffrey said, snapping out of a strange blank space where he had drifted for a moment.

"My best friend in prep school," said Pok, handing him an obituary notice with a photo of a young man in uniform.

"You knew this fellow?"

"Blood brothers," said Pok. "And now 'Killed In Action' it says. I'd like to go kill the assholes in Washington who sent him to 'Nam. And here's the real rip – Dan was part Arapaho, just like me. The Europeans came over here and stole the land right out from under his great-grandfather's moccasins, and then they ended up forcing Dan to go off and fight over in an entirely unjust war. I'll bet he just stopped and put down his gun when he realized that those Vietnamese he was fighting were exactly like him – natives defending their own land against outsiders from halfway around the world. Let me tell you, Roy, there's gonna be hell to pay, America has already accumulated one big radical pile of bad karma."

Suddenly Pok went stiff, on alert – he seemed to hear something outside the door. Jumping up, he walked on padded feet to the closet. In his stoned condition, Jeffrey thought Pok looked exactly like an Indian, with his long ponytail of black hair tied back with a red handkerchief. Pok disappeared into the closet a moment and came out with something that looked almost exactly like a real rifle. He worked the lever. Jeffrey gasped. It *was* a real rifle! Pok unlocked the door and opened it, pushing the rifle out into the hall, ready for action.

Suddenly the reality of the criminal situation struck Jeffrey like a bomb going off inside his chest. Here he was in Jonathan's room holding a half-smoked joint of genuine marijuana – enough incriminating evidence to send him to jail for twenty years in New Jersey. Holy Moses – what if his next phone call was to his parents from jail, asking them to cough up money for his bail? His mother would make him feel guilty enough to die. 'It started with those books, Jeffrey,' she would say. 'The boots, the long hair – and that hypnosis. What's this world coming to?'

Pok came back in, closed the door, locked it and put the rifle back in the closet. Then he sat down across from Jeffrey.

"Just the Bogeyman, I guess," he said. "Got to keep on your guard, though, there's CIA dudes all over campus these days. Hey Roy, you've let that joint die. You gotta keep atokin' if you wanta keep on smokin'. Here, I'll light it for you."

"Boy, my parents would die if they saw me now," said Jeffrey.

"Ah yes," Pok responded in a high voice in the middle of his own inhale, "the paranoia of the petrified patriarchs lives on in their offspring eternal. Listen to me, Jeffrey, look at me, come on, relax, there, breathe deep, okay now, everything's okay, no need to freak out, everything's just dandy, atta boy – here, have another toke."

Jeffrey watched the flame of the match dancing slowly, rhythmically in front of him. Suddenly from nowhere there were spots of light moving right at him, red spots, sunspots coming from outer space.

"... and I was locked up in Morocco last summer for two weeks before my father pulled connections to get me out ..."

"What?" said Jeffrey, whose faculties of critical examination were definitely somewhat diminished. Words sounded strange – wooooordzzz.

Fuzzzz . . . . buzzzzzzz . . . . wuzzzzzzz . . . .

"Hey look out, Jeffrey, the joint's going to burn your finger off!"

"Oh my god, Holy Moses!" Jeffrey jumped and dropped the burning cigarette right onto Jonathan's Oriental rug.

"Outa the way!" said Pok, retrieving the joint before it could do much damage. But there was a slight odor of burnt hair.

Suddenly the door of the room was opening. Jeffrey's heart decided to go on vacation for about five beats. In his somewhat altered state of consciousness he saw boots walking into the room, then he looked up along Levi legs to a familiar masculine face.

"Hey spaceman," said Jonathan, his words floating through the air in slow motion with bright colors flashing all around every word. In slow motion Jeffrey fell backwards and down onto a pile of pillows, ending up flat on his back, blissed out.

"I nosed you halfway down the stairs," Jonathan said to Pok. "You'd better be a little more cautious or the proctors are going to bust you. Next time, use a towel under the door and a little Right Guard in the air, hey?"

He sprayed deodorant outside the door for about five seconds to make sure that it would overpower the scent of the Holy Herb, and then closed and locked the door.

"So where have you been?" said Pok, ignoring Jonathan's scolding. "I was worried that you jumped off the bridge."

"I just hung out in New York last night, that's all," Jonathan said. "Hey, it looks like you're leading this fine young all-American scholar down the road to sin and degradation."

"You want a hit?" said Pok.

"No, no way," Jonathan replied. "I'm laying off that stuff semi-permanently, if you know what I mean."

"You mean your chick gave you a tough time and you're bummed out and dumping on everything."

"I mean my head's in enough trouble without adding any extra complications. What're you reading there?" Jonathan pointed to the Institute report.

"I found this on your desk," said Pok.

"Well maybe that's not for casual reading."

Jonathan went over and opened the window and climbed out onto the ledge, seeking a few breaths of high-altitude air.

Pok looked over at Jonathan's back. "So tell me what happened with Anne and I'll tell you that the Maharishi was a flame-out, okay?" he said.

Jonathan didn't reply. He just stood there breathing deeply. When he came back in he went over to his record collection and selected some music. Jefferson Airplane: 'You Gotta Find Somebody to Love.'

"What a crazy night," Jonathan uttered over the rock music. "I should have stayed with you and meditated with the Maharishi."

"So did Anne give you the bounce?"

"Other way around. I was a total asshole, I think I really blew it."

"So where've you been all night?"

"Oh, wherever. I dropped in on a chick I used to know in the city, crashed on her couch. Anyway, about that Institute report –"

"Ease up, I'm not going to turn you in for stealing it," said Pok.

Jonathan took it from Pok's lap, quickly looked through it, then tossed it aside. "What the hell," he said, "there's nothing in it that means much."

"That's because maybe you didn't read it carefully. Did you notice who controls the purse strings? Our Deputy Director, Dr. Carl Pfeiffer. I didn't know he's the Secretary-Treasurer for the whole place. He's got those big vials of LSD left over from that study where he gave acid to prisoners."

"And he's not the only one with vials of acid," said Jonathan. "I hear from Mike that they've got enough acid tucked away somewhere at the Institute to turn on everyone in Washington D.C. Pure Sandoz quart bottles."

"So where'd you find the report?"

"Mike left it laying around, I scored it when he wasn't looking. I'll drop it back on his desk tomorrow and nobody will know. I was hoping for something more dramatic."

Jeffrey suddenly sat upright, blinked and said, "Uhm, where am I?"

"Home base, Roy, glad to see you up and kicking," said Pok. "Where did you float off to?"

"I saw lights," Jeffrey replied.

"Lights?" Pok said, interested.

"Coming right at me, it was amazing, totally amazing."

"Were they round lights, flashing on and off so fast you could hardly see them flashing?"

"Sort of, and God help me, here they come again," Jeffrey said, as his eyes rolled up into his head. "They're coming right at me, help me!"

Jonathan quickly went into action, kneeling beside Jeffrey, putting a hand on his shoulder. "It's okay, Jeffrey, just relax, you're just hallucinating, you can let go of it if you want."

"No," said Pok. "Stay with it, Jeffrey. Tell me what you're seeing. What color are the lights?"

"Red and blue."

"Open yourself to them," Pok said, caught up in the excitement of the moment. "See if the lights are bringing you a communication. Let them leave their message."

Jonathan fired a warning glance at Pok and then turned his attention to Jeffrey. "Just relax and feel free to open your eyes whenever you want," he said.

"Let him go into it," Pok said. "You're crazy if you cut off a contact from EBE's."

"EBE's?" said Jeffrey.

"Extraterrestrial Biological Entities," explained Pok.

"Pok. You're stoned and playing with Jeffrey's mind and I don't like it," said Jonathan.

"He's tapped into the Space Brothers and you're trying to pull him out of communication. That's nuts. The Beatles tuned into that message, that's why their vibrations are astral. You don't tune in, so you don't know they're out there."

"Pok, please, back off – let him have his own experience."

Jeffrey sat up and smiled. "Hello. I'm back," he said.

The phone rang. Jeffrey reacted as if he were being electrocuted. "Don't worry," said Pok. "It's not your momma."

Jonathan stared at him a very long moment, then picked up the phone. "Hello?"

Meanwhile: "Hey, Roy, have you ever gone down to the soccer field to look for flying saucers?" said Pok.

"Flying sausages," said Jeffrey. "No, I haven't."

"Boy, are you gone," said Pok. "Must be a good buzz."

Just as Pok said the word 'buzz,' that exact sensation shot up Jeffrey's spine, exploding instantly into his brain.

"Buzzzzz," said Jeffrey. "Shmuzzzz. Fuzzzzz. Duzzz."

"C'mon, Jeffrey, keep it down, okay? I can't hear over the phone," said Jonathan.

"Getting you stoned is my current project in patriotism, Roy," said Pok. "The purpose of this lesson is to teach you the mystic ways of George Washington. He used to smoke grass as a cure for the common cold. He thought puff was the ultimate cure for everything – until the Establishment came down on his head and he had to switch back to booze."

"Come on, Pok, would you turn off the bullshit tap for a minute?" said Jonathan, in a very irritated tone of voice. "I can hardly hear a word Anne's saying."

"Forgive me brother," said Pok, hanging his head in shame, "for I have sinned."

"Well yeah, sure – and I'm glad you called," Jonathan said into the phone. "Like I said, I was going to call you. I don't know what happened last night, I went loony. It was some condition I was carrying from the loony-bin I think – anyway, thanks for not dumping on me totally. I really mean that. Sorry. Listen," Jonathan went on, "that's perfect, I really mean it. No, I've been thinking about it, too, and I'm really sure. I'll meet you at the bus stop, pack a big suitcase. I'll look for a place."

Princeton University reunion

Princeton University reunion alongside the Whig Cliosophic Society, the Princeton debating society founded by James Madison and Aaron Burr

14. Ring Around the Moon

The Institute parties every month or so were a big event everyone looked forward to – a chance to hang out with each other off Institute grounds, which meant that none of the formal Institute rules were in effect. Bernie only invited people he felt wouldn't be upset about a few joints going around through the room. Naturally, Jonathan was always included in the circle of intimates that met at Mike's place out in the woods for the monthly gathering.

As he drove along the back road that wound its way toward Mike's well-hidden cabin, Jonathan was wondering why he felt so nervous this time. Anne was with him, but what the hell? He had always brought chicks to the party before, why was he so nervous about showing up and letting Bernie meet his girl for the first time? It felt sort of like taking a girl home to the ranch for his dad to judge, like quality horse-flesh.

Two barking dogs ran over to attack as the MG pulled in among a dozen cars already assembled. Jonathan spotted Bernie's Chevy at once.

"Dumb dogs, I've been out here fifty times, and they always go through the same routine," he said to Anne. "Dad would shoot them and good riddance if they were ranch dogs. No brains at all."

He killed the engine and suddenly the dogs stopped barking, leaving the two of them surrounded by an eerie silence. The stone cabin was actually little more than one huge room that someone had built ages ago as a weekend retreat. Smoke was coming from the chimney as they walked up the path.

"They're friendly dogs," Anne said, approaching the mutts to pet them. Anne was an animal lover and eager to find new friends of the canine species. A moment later Jonathan found himself playing with the damned dogs, too, grinning and talking to them as if they were big babies.

"Jonathan, there you are," said a loud voice from the direction of the house.

"Ah, uhm, Mike, how's it going? This is my good friend, Anne, who I told you about."

With Mike's entrance routine self-activated, Anne made the rounds of people near the door first. It was a big party this time, not one of the more intimate touchy-feely encounter groups, and Jonathan was glad for that. He'd seen enough sexual situations at these parties to know that he was the only uptight cowboy among the hypnosis gang. But he'd come a long way since he had arrived at Princeton with a virgin groin and Puritan ethics.

"Uhm, Anne, this is one of the hypnotists at the Institute, Randy Vokies," said Jonathan, and then "Art, I'd like you to meet a friend of mine, Anne," and "Hey, Kelly, how's it going, when did you get back from San Francisco? This is Anne, she's just moved out here from there."

In all there were now six hypnotists working at the Institute, some of them part-time like Jonathan, and then there were a couple of secretaries, the librarian, research assistants and a dozen or so subjects who were trusted enough to attend parties of this sort without spreading rumors.

Jonathan was beginning to tire of the introduction scene just as Bernie suddenly appeared from the kitchen area with a plate that seemed to be covered with seaweed.

"Ah, uhm, Anne, this is Bernie – Bernie, my good friend, Anne."

"Well," he said. "It's good to see you finally, Anne. Jonathan has told me all about you. How are you liking New York?"

"Oh, well, actually, not too much, I just moved to Princeton, in fact," she said. Jonathan tensed as she let the secret slip.

"Oh, really, that's interesting," Bernie went on, firing a glance at Jonathan. "What are you going to be doing?"

"Well, I'm going to paint for fun and just find some job to get by for a while," she said. "Jonathan found me a perfect little studio apartment in town."

"Hmmm."

Jonathan could sense Bernie's displeasure with the situation, even though Anne detected only friendship.

"Well, if we can be of any help," said Bernie, "you know where to turn – any friend of Jonathan's is certainly a part of my circle. By the way, the wok is still warming up but can I get you some of these delicious macrobiotic hors d'oeuvres? Or some herb tea?"

"Oh, I'd just like some juice," she said. "But I can get it myself."

"I'll help you find a glass," said Bernie. "What would you like, Jonathan?"

"Triple Jose Cuervo," he said for the hell of it, and relaxed as Anne went off with Bernie.

There were no chairs or sofas at all at Mike's, you were either on your feet or down on a pillow or mattress – a handy arrangement for later on, when everybody would be puffing the Holy Herb and fooling around.

The dogs started barking again as a car came driving up to the house. A few moments later Jeffrey walked in with Linda who was wearing one of her see-through blouses.

"Uhm, gee, what a neat place for a party," said Jeffrey. "This is a really hip scene – but that dirt road to this cabin was really murder on Linda's car."

"Oh, look who's here – it's Matt! I didn't know you were back," Linda said excitedly, as she spotted her old buddy and hopped over seated bodies to get to him. Jeffrey winced as he watched Linda kiss Matt on the mouth with her soft red lips. It was a French kiss no less.

"What happened to your hair!" said Linda. "Oh my God, Matt, they didn't get you, did they?"

Matt shrugged his broad shoulders. "Afraid so," he said.

"Oh, shit – so when do you leave for boot camp?"

"Eight days."

"Total bummer. I thought Bernie was going to get you a draft-deferred status, isn't that –"

Bernie was suddenly right in the middle of the conversation. "Don't everybody get upset about Matt just yet," he said in his smooth, confident voice that had just a touch of whine in its controlled tenor. "Just this afternoon I was on the phone with a lawyer in Washington who has the right connections. I don't think they're going to get Matt after all. Right, Matt?"

Matt shrugged his shoulders again. He was the sort of guy who would take whatever came his way in life without complaint, a good old Hindu at heart, especially after his two years at the Institute. "Whatever's happening is happening, where's that joint? I know I saw one somewhere."

Matt had been an Institute hypnotist who, rather than hiding from the draft under Bernie's protective umbrella, had gone back to graduate school to study for a Ph.D. in psychology at the University of Michigan.

Jonathan and Anne fell into some small-talk with Jeffrey, who had latched onto them just as soon as Linda disappeared with Matt.

"You have interesting hands," Anne said to Jeffrey.

"What, my hands? Oh, they're okay for hands, I guess."

"Can I study them?" Anne asked. "I like to match hands with faces when I meet people."

"Oh, sure, I guess so," he said, somewhat embarrassed. He glanced at Jonathan to make sure it was okay to do something so personal with his hypnotist's girlfriend. When Jonathan didn't react, he gave Anne his hands hurriedly, like they were a pair of old shoes or something.

She held his hands lightly in her own and looked quietly at the lines on the palms, then glanced up to his face, making Jeffrey blush.

"Bernie made me a suggestion," she said to Jonathan as an aside, as she studied Jeffrey's hands.

"Oh?"

"He says one of the secretaries is on a leave of absence, and he needs someone to type up a speech that he's giving at the American Psychological Association conference in San Antonio next week."

"And?" said Jonathan, tensing.

"He offered me the job, starting Monday, and maybe some more secretarial work after. What do you think?"

Jonathan was instantly suspicious of Bernie's show of friendship. The idea of having Anne working at the Institute seemed bizarre, and the fact that Bernie suggested it seemed totally out of character. Jonathan glanced up and found Bernie looking at him right at that moment – it was the kind of coincidence that happened often at these parties. Synchronicity, Bernie called it, a term for extreme coincidences invented by Sigmund Freud's rebellious protégé Carl Jung.

Bernie was staring at Jonathan with those haunting eyes in a very possessive way that Jonathan reacted against instantly –

but maybe, Jonathan reminded himself, Bernie was right in saying that Jonathan was overly defensive, still half-caught in old uptight cowboy reactions.

"Uhm, are you done with these?" Jeffrey said, sensing that the entire party was watching Anne holding his hands.

"Oh," she said, tuning in to him again. She gave Jeffrey's hands a friendly squeeze and released them. "Maybe sometime I could draw your hands."

"Just my hands? Well, sure, why not? Anytime. Maybe when you're working out at the Institute."

"Did you say yes?" Jonathan asked Anne in a low tone.

She cocked her head slightly as she tried to read his expression. "You don't seem to want me to say yes."

"Well, it just seems a little strange," Jonathan replied, not wanting to discuss the situation in front of Jeffrey. But when he glanced at Jeffrey, he saw that Jeffrey was busy watching Linda, who had just made a reappearance from outside with Matt. Linda's hair and see-through blouse were mussed, and Jonathan could tell that Jeffrey was feeling rejected and crestfallen.

Anne found Jonathan's hand, and the slight pressure she exerted indicated her desire to stand up. Without thinking, he responded. They walked off to a corner that was relatively empty of ears.

"Listen," he said, "do you really want to work at the Institute? From everything you've always said about the place, you probably won't dig the scene at all. What do you think of Bernie, anyway?"

"I don't know. The way he related to me sexually was certainly curious."

"How so?"

"I think he's more attracted to you than to me," said Anne.

Jonathan contemplated her remark and gulped the last swallow of his drink, which Bernie had modified into tequila and water. "When I first met Bernie I thought he was a genius of sorts," said Jonathan. "And he took me in like I was important, or like I had the potential to be somebody very important someday. He did a lot of therapy with me, hypnotherapy of course – but these days, what with all the erasure of memory and such, I don't know – I look at him and feel—"

"Feel what?"

"Well, nauseous, actually."

She grimaced and looked away. "Well still, I think I'll take some work at the Institute if you don't mind, it's all so interesting." She looked back at him. "And after all, it's what you do."

"Yeah, it's what I do if I want to stay out of the army when I graduate."

"I don't get it, Jonathan. Why does that work get you a deferment from the army?"

"There are parts of it that are top secret. 'In the national interest,' was Bernie's term for it. I've begun to suspect a CIA connection, actually."

"The CIA? That sounds so paranoid, Jonathan."

"Well, maybe it's not. There are some pretty strange guys who pop up here and there and like to warn people not to talk about what we do out there. Anyway, I could split the whole scene entirely – and if they tried to draft me to fight in Vietnam, I could go to Mexico with Pok. My big brother phoned me last night to tell me he has some friends down in Baja I could stay with – I don't really know about any of this, actually – right now everything's so foggy."

Mike popped out from the kitchen and announced that the wok was sizzling with goodies, and herd instinct overtook nearly everyone in the room, including Anne.

But Jonathan reacted against the herd, once again feeling the nausea that had been plaguing him for weeks now, months even. Tonight he felt out of tune with these psychology nuts, he felt pissed off at Anne, he just wanted some breathing space, everybody was pressing in on him and he felt that he was going to suffocate if he didn't get out of that cabin immediately. So he put his glass down on a windowsill and headed out the door, hoping no one would see him make his exit.

The air outside was much cooler and free of smoke, but still he felt as if he were going to throw up as he walked along the path from the house. The two dogs followed him until he growled and stomped loud enough to convince them to leave him alone.

The moon was full, and there was enough light for taking a walk even where the path went under trees. Jonathan went about a long way up the path and then sat down, feeling better being distant from the house. But someone was coming up the path after him, goddamnit. He knew it would be Anne, and right then he didn't want to have her around him at all. She was the cause of his freak-out, he knew it – she was pushing herself right into every pocket of his life and leaving him no space at all. It was no good. He was going to tell her that he didn't like the idea of her working at the Institute, that he didn't like her living in Princeton, and that he was about ready to blow.

But it was Jeffrey. "Uhm, I hope I'm not disturbing you," he said when he got closer.

"Hey, no problem."

"What a moon!"

"Yeah, I was just checking it out. Nice ring around it. Who knows what that may indicate."

"Mind if I have a seat?" Jeffrey asked.

"Help yourself."

"Boy, your girlfriend is really pretty."

"Yeah, she's okay."

"It'll be fun having her out at the Institute."

"Barrel of laughs," said Jonathan in a very sarcastic tone.

"You don't sound very positive about it."

"Listen, Jeffrey, you're so blindly eager be a part of this scene here that you don't seem to see the whammo waiting for you – but then neither did I."

"Whammo?"

"You think it's a lot of fun, playing with the conditions I'm giving you."

"It's the most amazing experience of my life. Every time I go out to the Institute for a session with you, I –"

"I'm just saying that maybe you should take a more careful look at situations before you plow into them head-first."

"I still don't know what you mean."

"So forget it. Maybe we should quit head-tripping for a while and just meditate, okay?"

"Uhm – okay, sure. Hey, I forgot to tell you something important. Something amazing. There's a senior Pok knows who is selling his car. It's pretty beat up and it has a hundred thirty thousand miles, so this senior's father is buying him a brand new one. And since I'm working at the Institute regularly and transportation is a hassle, my parents are letting me buy it."

"Buy what?" said Jonathan.

"Weren't you even listening? The old car."

"I thought we agreed to stop head-tripping and meditate."

"Okay, if you insist," said Jeffrey. "But that's great news, isn't it? About the car? From Pok's friend."

Jonathan didn't reply. His eyes were closed as he sat there cross-legged in the cold on rocky ground and tried to create a silence within himself – but volcanoes, geysers, fountains, streams and rushing rivers of thoughts and feelings came gushing to the surface of Jonathan's mind. He opened his mouth without thinking and what came out was a low "ommmm..."

Jeffrey joined in, almost inaudibly at first, but then their voices gained in strength. And then Jonathan started chanting, wailing like an American Indian – it was an Arapaho death chant that Pok had taught him last week, and it brought into his consciousness all the horrors and pain of the past – Indians slaughtered, Japanese pulverized by the atomic bomb; Germans, Italians, French, English dismembered and crushed, Jews gassed, Vietnamese napalmed, John F. Kennedy with a gaping bullet hole in his brain, Gandhi on his burning funeral pyre, Jesus on his bloody cross....

Slowly, the chant faded away, and they opened their eyes.

"That was really strange," said Jeffrey. "Where'd you learn to chant?"

"Pok taught me."

"Jonathan, can I ask you something, er, really personal?"

"Fire away."

"It's, uhm, well, about Linda. You, uhm, you had a thing with her last year?"

"Guess so."

"Well, I don't know, I was just wondering, you know, well, I don't know how to say it."

"It's like this, Jeffrey, enjoy what's there, and don't look for what isn't. That's life in a nutshell."

"Look," said Jeffrey, "there's someone coming up the trail."

"Judging by the waddle, I think that it's Bernie."

"Tell me, does Dr. Osmond sometimes come to these parties?" Jeffrey asked. "I don't see him tonight."

"No way, he's straight-laced socially, sexually. He'd blow a gasket if he came out here."

"Isn't it amazing that Dr. Osmond and Bernie have so many incredible people working on their projects? Mike's house might have half of the future top psychologists in the country in it right now. I mean, it's unbelievable how I just happened to see that announcement that day and then applied to be a subject. I was thinking that hypnosis would help me with my studies and, well, with girls. I had no idea it was the gateway to nirvana. In fact, now that I think of it, I didn't even know what nirvana was until I –"

"Hey," Jonathan interrupted, watching Bernie arrive. "You don't know a damn what nirvana is yet – like Pok says, wait until someone holds you under for the count." He glanced up. "Hi, Bernie, what's happening?"

"Oh, there you are," said Bernie, huffing and puffing from the walk. "It's freezing out here, Jonathan, where's your coat?"

"Feels warm to me, isn't it warm to you?"

"Jonathan, could we talk?"

"Talk away."

"Jeffrey, would you mind letting us talk alone?"

"Oh, sure, of course, I was just going back, I want to get some more food, I love oriental food. Well, see you later. Bye Jonathan."

And he was gone.

Bernie was wearing an expensive coat with a fur collar, and he took it off and put it around Jonathan's shoulders. Jonathan rejected the gesture with a quick shrug, and the coat fell off onto the ground. Bernie picked it up.

"Jonathan, what's wrong, tell me," he said, ignoring Jonathan's rejection and sitting down alongside him.

"Nothing wrong with me. What's wrong with you?"

"Me?"

"How come you offered Anne a job at the Institute, what's up? I don't like it."

"Don't tell me that you're even suspicious of that."

"I know you don't like me hanging out with her."

"What makes you say such a thing?" asked Bernie.

"I can tell."

"I like Anne, she's intelligent and pretty, and she seems very much in love with you. So why shouldn't we welcome her into our circle?"

"Maybe I don't want her in 'our circle.'"

"Why not?"

"Hey, I didn't come here tonight to talk group dynamics."

Bernie sighed. "Jonathan, everything I do to try to make us closer, you reject. Why is it? I'm not ashamed of the fact that I sometimes think of you as if you were my own son. But every time I do something that should bring us together, you push me away."

"Jesus, Bernie, all I'm saying is that you were totally down on my relationship with Lucy. Now you're acting totally positive toward Anne. But I know what's going on in your head. You think Anne is a negative influence on me."

"But just the opposite is true. I think you made the right decision in asking her to move to Princeton. You need a woman to be close to you. That was what you were always talking about when, well, during a couple of sessions when I was helping you to explore what –"

"– Stop it," snapped Jonathan, cutting Bernie off. "I'm fed up to here with your fucking hypnotic bullshit, I've had it. All those blank spaces, with you knowing everything about me, prying into my brain while I'm totally gone to the world – I don't think it's right. I think my dad's right – nobody has the right to mess with people's minds, not even you."

Strained silence. Jonathan thought of his father, so totally distant from him now – maybe walking outside the ranch house ... the moon would just be rising, three thousand miles away.

"Jonathan, I know the last year has been hard for you. I put you through a great deal with those new conditions Humphry developed. And maybe you're right, maybe I push limits too far. And yes, maybe I haven't been completely transparent with you. But believe me – you and I have gone to the ultimate reaches of consciousness together, during your sessions."

"Bernie, you're a maniac. Damn, it's freezing out here. Tell me something – you and Mike, what's going on between you?"

"What?"

"You heard me."

"Ah yes. Jonathan and his Puritan ethic again."

"I want to know," said Jonathan.

"Know what?"

"Are you and Mike getting it on? I saw you kiss him last week."

Bernie laughed. "You mean that time in the kitchen at the Institute? That was just a simple demonstration to test how bystanders react when people break sexual taboos in public. You didn't think that –" He laughed again, he seemed to find Jonathan's question amusing.

"You think I don't remember anything you did to me during our sessions."

"You don't, of course. But I'm planning on restoring your memories of everything, believe me –"

"I don't believe anything anymore. I have no idea what you're doing when I'm in a trance. But I do remember you touching me during a session. Sort of a vague memory, maybe, but I'm sure I remember you touching me."

"Oh, well yes, I did in fact, it was part of my attempt to get you to progress beyond your childhood fears of touching. That's a normal therapeutic technique, and you responded well. When did you remember that?"

"I don't know, awhile back."

"What else did you remember?"

"Nothing that I remember now."

"Well maybe we should do some special sessions to –"

"Damn, Bernie, that's just what's getting to me and you know it. You said I was going to be completely free of being a subject once we finished with the conditions, but you –"

"Jonathan, you are free of the conditions now. All we have to do is explore what happens for the six months following the conditions, and then you are free to –"

"But I want to be free now."

"You and I both know that you have a tendency to rebel against our work – but we weather through those times. We will again now. What a beautiful moon, we've been talking so much that I hardly noticed it. Look at that ring around it."

"Bernie, will you promise that I'll get a draft deferment if I keep working as a hypnotist next year, after I graduate?"

"Of course, I'll do my best. Our research is considered to be in the national interest – they've never drafted my staff members. And I'll do my best to keep Anne busy with work too, so we can have her as part of the family. Right now there's nothing at all that's threatening to you. Here we are, life is flowing well, all is okay, you have your girlfriend, and you have a draft-deferred job. You can fully relax here and enjoy the circle around the moon. Okay?"

Jonathan stood up and exhaled loudly into the night air, sending white mist out in a sudden stream. "Okay," he said.

Back at Anne's apartment a little later, she put on some music: Debussy's "Afternoon of a Faun."

"Why don't we turn off the lamp?" she suggested. "It would be beautiful with just the candlelight."

Jonathan went over and switched it off. The room took on a warm glow from the flickering candle. Anne sat down on the edge of her bed and bent over to unlace her boots. He sat down on a meditation pillow and pulled off his own boots. They both took off their socks at the same time and then looked up at each other and smiled. And then Anne crossed her arms and grasped the hem of her sweater with both hands and slowly raised the sweater up over her stomach and then over her breasts and then over her head. She smiled and tossed the sweater to him.

But when he stood up to go to her, suddenly he felt dizzy. Everything in the room seemed flat. Anne looked unreal, like a two-dimensional poster, and the walls and ceiling seemed to be closing in on him. For a moment he thought he was going to black out.

But then Anne was touching him, kissing him. He held on desperately to the stimulating sensations of the smoothness of her warm naked body as she caressed him, the gentle warmth of her hands bringing him back to reality as her fingers slipped under his shirt ...

about collecting damning
he medical torture practices
countries deemed to be
e United States. The case
: it to trial. The plaintiffs
1 of $100,000 each which
hem on the understanding
never publicly discuss the

listed above only became
: because of the public's
Senate investigations, and
researchers under the
rmation Act. Today, in
itry in the world, torture
nipulation of the human
on someone every single
s have become so
ven victims who become
aware of what, or who,
with their minds. The
in use today are more
eadly than ever before.
nowing just how many
, or perhaps more
ment operations, are
e present time. Perhaps
f attitude by many of
on the ground in the
uld be related to the
long-range behaviour
s.

ch conducted by the
has inspired both the
ity and the Defense
look at the potential
for covert psychic

blishing this story is
you. It is to remind
veil of secrecy that
nal security", there
ing mind-control
eve you of your self

> In all there were 149 MKUltra subprojects dealing with behavioural modification. A further 33 subprojects were funded under MKUltra that were not related to this type of research. We will never know what these projects were about.

CIA Mind Control Research

15. Nobody's Trained Monkey

Coach glared as Jonathan walked in ten minutes late to the fencing team pre-meet protein lunch of steak, peas and potatoes. Jonathan sat down and ate voraciously, arguing for extra helpings which the rules said he couldn't have. He finally got another steak.

Then came the usual gung-ho pep talk from Coach Sieja, and after that a couple hours off to digest and prepare mentally – focusing the mind totally on winning-winning-winning for the team! Then they were back at the gym suiting up in their white cotton outfits with thick material to keep the opponents' stabs from hurting too much. They wore high socks, striped Princeton orange and black, folded down right below the knee and taped so they would stay up.

Anne had eaten dinner at Tower Club with Wayne and Glen, and when Jonathan got upstairs they were all in the bleachers, along with several hundred other people who were all waiting for the tournament against N.Y.U. to begin. Although everyone on the team was suited up, only nine of them would be fencing in the tournament. Coach had everyone suit up for home meets, so they would look impressive to all the other college teams who usually only brought eleven or twelve men.

The first round of bouts was called – foil, epée and then sabre. The loudspeaker called Jonathan for the first foil bout. He went out onto the mat and hooked up his foil to the cord that went to the electric machine that scored the points. Then he stood with his helmet under his arm and saluted his opponent and the director of the bout. The fencer he was competing against in the initial bout seemed young and relatively inexperienced – perhaps even a bit scared.

"Pret?" the director called out.

Jonathan put on his helmet and nodded that he was ready. He focused all his concentration on his opponent on the mat.

"Commence!" came the French order to begin. Jonathan shouted a wild war whoop and advanced toward his opponent threateningly. His opponent retreated – but then suddenly counter-attacked. With a fast stroke of his sword, Jonathan cleared his blade, lunged with a flash and touched him right under his elbow on his left side.

One touch.

When the action started again, his opponent crammed his blade into Jonathan's ribs in a wild attack. It hurt and made him mad, so Jonathan went to work and finished him off, not bothering to try to use his Zen technique because it was easy enough to defeat him with the European method.

His second bout twenty minutes later was a closer battle. Jonathan had to work hard for his points, out-thinking his opponent, knowing that errors in judgment of a tenth of an inch would mean a touch against him. Coach was watching him silently, judgmentally – he could detect that Jonathan was now letting go of the strategy Coach had laid out for him against this opponent. Instead, Jonathan was concentrating on totally quieting his mind in the present moment, just watching his breathing and waiting for the first Zen flash of the day to hit.

Suddenly it did. He felt a flash of psychic electricity run through him and he lunged and touched his opponent. The N.Y.U. coach called time and went out onto the mat to talk with his fencer. Jonathan's coach came over to him and patted him on the shoulder. Good touch, he said, but remember his double parry, and then the bout was on again.

The opposing fencer played around some more, then made an attack. Jonathan took his blade and touched him again. Jonathan was beginning to feel it inside. The Zen Method. It was right; it was working.

The Director asked Jonathan if he was ready. Jonathan nodded, and the action began again. Jonathan stood still, waiting. His opponent lunged and touched him.

Next point, same thing.

Jonathan was just waiting for the Zen flash to come again. His coach started yelling at him from the sidelines to wake up but Jonathan ignored him. He felt confident, he knew what he was doing. He was sure he could win if he just stuck to his new method and waited for the next flash to hit.

The action started again and the flash came and Jonathan scored a lightning touch. He won the final two points the same way. This was it. He was a Zen fencer now. His European period was over.

As he got unhooked from the electric scoring equipment, he could see Coach glaring at him from the team bench. He'd let a fencer score two clean touches against him without even parrying to defend himself. He had committed a sacrilege.

He ignored Coach and went over to the drinking fountain, took a sip of water and spat it out. He was going to fight this tournament his own way, no matter what Coach thought. He wasn't Coach's trained monkey or his dad's trained monkey or the Institute's trained monkey. He didn't need anyone pressuring him or ordering him around or hypnotizing him. He was his own man.

He returned to the team bench and watched while Marty Rubinstein, the best N.Y.U. fencer, won his second bout against Tod, five-to-zero. Tod had three or four slightly vulnerable weak spots in his defense technique, and Rubinstein took full advantage of them.

After beating Tod, Rubinstein went over to his team bench opposite Princeton's, sat down and waited for his bout with Jonathan to come up. Their eyes met several times, and each time, Rubinstein smiled. Jonathan wasn't sure what his smile meant. The last time Jonathan had fenced him, at the Nationals the year before, Rubinstein had placed first and Jonathan had placed fifth. Jonathan knew the smile wasn't innocent friendship.

"Jonathan?"

He turned around. It was Coach. "I want to talk with you," Coach said.

"Talk away."

"Not here. Downstairs."

With no patience for what he knew was about to take place, Jonathan followed Coach downstairs to the locker room. Coach closed the door.

"Jonathan, you're making a fool of both of us. Do you realize you stood out there on the mat and you let those fencers score touches against you without even raising your blade in defense?"

"Coach, I've tried to explain to you the technique I'm using but you don't listen."

"Listen to what? I know when somebody is letting me down."

"Look, Coach, I can't handle anyone else on my back, I've had it up to here," Jonathan told him. "I've had enough pressure and guilt – I'm living my own life now, I'm nobody's trained monkey."

"I've devoted my life to this sport," Coach came right back at him, "and you're treating it like a frivolous pastime. I'm just asking you not to make fools of us – please, remember how I taught you to fence against Rubinstein. You owe us at least that much. Stop fooling around long enough to lead your team to victory."

"If you want to pull me out and not have me fence Rubinstein, fine, go ahead – but if I'm fencing, I'm going to do it my own way."

"You know I'm not going to pull you out. But get your mind out of the fog and concentrate!"

Jonathan went running up the stairs to the fencing balcony. Anne was someplace in the crowd but he didn't look for her. As he sat down on the team bench he found himself trembling. Damn. He had to get centered, do some breathing exercises – somehow get focused again so he could shift into the Zen state of mind and win the crucial bout. The meet had progressed to the point where Jonathan would win it for Princeton if he beat Marty Rubinstein.

He let his eyes glance around the stands. He noticed Jeffrey up in the bleachers, squirming, nervous with anticipation. He kept scanning the rows until he saw Anne. He met her eyes – ah, that felt better. She smiled warmly and he returned her smile. Now he was feeling slightly elated, light-headed, and there was a slow tingling sensation coming up his spine into the back of his neck. His arms felt as if they were growing longer. Then out of the blue he remembered that strange sensation of flapping his wings and flying into freedom – flying away and never returning.

Glancing back at the stands, Jonathan suddenly thought he saw one of those two guys who had taunted him staring right back at him – one of the CIA guys or whoever they were – but then he was gone. And then he caught a glimpse of Bernie in the stands. But that was impossible. Bernie didn't come to fencing tournaments.

At that moment the loudspeaker called him for the deciding bout with Marty Rubinstein. Tod came out personally to make sure Jonathan's electric equipment was hooked up correctly. Stay in the present, thought Jonathan. Focus on breathing. Trust the Zen flow.

Rubinstein pranced around at the other end of the mat while his men hooked him up. The referee balanced the official two-ounce weight on the tip of each of their electric foils to make sure they would take the correct amount of pressure to score a touch on the electric scoring equipment. Then Rubinstein and Jonathan stood back and saluted each other. Jonathan felt better – cowboy tough, almost angry suddenly. Angry at everybody but Anne, and ready to fight.

"Pret?" the director called out.

Jonathan put on his helmet and nodded.

"Commence!"

He took a deep breath, slowly exhaled and stood there calmly while Rubinstein pranced around in front of him, going through mock attacks and mock retreats, trying to get Jonathan to respond with a counter-attack. When Rubinstein advanced and threatened, Jonathan retreated, not wanting to make his move until he felt the Zen flash.

'And when you awaken, Jonathan, you will be six inches tall.'

Jonathan glanced to the audience again, searching for Bernie's eyes. Rubinstein backed Jonathan off the mat. Twice off would be a point against him.

Jonathan was struggling to maintain his size, fighting to ward off the condition and not become smaller right there on the mat.

Goddamn you Bernie –

They returned to the center and the action started again. Rubinstein backed Jonathan off the mat and a point was registered against him for giving ground. He heard Coach shout at him but he didn't pay any attention to him. The Director said "Commence!" and they were fencing again.

Rubinstein lunged at him and Jonathan retreated. Then Jonathan raised his foil and aimed it directly at his opponent as they faced each other without moving. Jonathan knew Rubinstein was out to get him, he could feel it.

'Just relax, Jonathan, you are now the calm and crystal sea, the void, the eternal flow ... infinite ...'

Breathe, damnit! His chest was so tight –

Hee-up, goddamn! Rubinstein had touched him. A simple one-two attack.

"Pret?"

Jonathan wasn't ready but he nodded anyway and the action was on again. Rubinstein looked like a Medieval Crusader with his helmet covering his entire head – a phantom marauder ... an executioner ... the Bogeyman.

As Rubinstein attacked, Jonathan reacted with a wide parry and a quick retreat. He backed Jonathan up. Jonathan went off the mat again. Another point against him.

They were brought back to the starting line and they began again. Rubinstein immediately attacked with a fleche and touched Jonathan. "Zero-to-four," the scorekeeper chanted.

Coach came out onto the mat. He pounded his fist against Jonathan's helmet and shouted something.

"Get off my mat, Coach," said Jonathan quietly. "Get off my mat and leave me alone." The compressed anger felt good. Coach slowly backed away, his face red, his eyes glaring. The gymnasium was deathly quiet.

Jonathan looked out into the crowd for Anne, but all he could see was staring hostile faces.

"Pret?"

Jonathan nodded. Rubinstein nodded.

"Commence!"

Rubinstein attacked – a long, swift, low attack, trying to catch Jonathan instantly and end the bout. Jonathan parried hard, almost knocking Rubinstein's sword from his hand. That felt good too – tough the way he used to be when he wrestled a steer to the ground. His fighting spirit was back. Rubinstein attacked again, a complex attack with an advance to gain better scoring distance. But with each threatening attack of his blade, Jonathan instantly responded with a sharp parry, the Zen energy growing hot inside him. They fenced rougher and rougher, harder and harder, neither of them giving ground.

Then came an explosion of light – release – Jonathan was soaring hundreds of feet high, to where he could see the lake on the Institute grounds. 'I am your lifeline,' said Bernie. 'You are leaving your physical body –'

So quickly that Jonathan never saw it coming, Rubinstein attacked him like a flash of lightning and touched him cleanly on the chest.

Silence from the crowd.

Then bursts of cheering for Rubinstein.

N.Y.U. had won.

Down in the locker room, feeling angry and alone, Jonathan ignored the tense hostility of his teammates, and instead in desperation he focused on locating his disconnected body beneath his numb head. Then outside the gym, with Anne at his side, they were walking along in the moonlight, not even glancing at one another.

"I'm sorry you lost," she said.

"It doesn't matter," he said.

The wind was just sharp enough to feel crisp. He put his hands in his pockets and watched his boots walking below him. When he glanced over at Anne she smiled back a little too intensely, as if anxious to talk or relate somehow, but Jonathan just wanted to get centered inside himself.

"How about we take a drive?" he said.

"Where do you want to go?"

"Nowhere in particular – just away."

"Sure, if you want."

At the parking lot, he opened the car door for her and met her gaze. She reached behind his head and pulled him to her. Their lips met, then their tongues. Then he pulled away, went over to the driver's side, jumped in and started the engine – jammed it into first and buzzed out of the parking lot at breakneck speed, tires squealing, accelerating down the road toward the bridge over Princeton Lake.

But just before he got to the bridge his eyes blurred with tears, forcing him to slam on the brakes and pull off to the side of the road. "Goddamn, Goddamn them all," he muttered. He tried to hold back his emotions, but his throat was so convulsed he felt as though he was going to throw up – and then suddenly his emotions broke through and he just sat there and sobbed and sobbed. His eyes were running streams of tears and sobs were coming involuntarily out of his mouth, and all the while Anne was there with him, telling him, "Go ahead, it's all right to cry, we all need to cry sometimes – even cowboys."

TAKING LIBERTIES

CIA Mind Control Experiments

Agency Reneges on Promise to Victims

BY JOHN HANRAHAN

Despite promises last summer by CIA Director Admiral Stansfield Turner, the federal government thus far has formulated no program to locate persons who served as unwitting guinea pigs in the CIA's MK ULTRA mind control experiments in the 1950s and 60s.

The MK ULTRA program spanned two decades and involved at least 149 projects conducted throughout the country in 86 colleges, universities and private medical facilities, and in various everyday situations. The projects, which supposedly ended in 1973, included research and human experimentation in such areas as electroshock, psychosurgery, mind-altering drugs and biological agents.

Some 429 experiments were conducted on psychotics and nonpsychotics with a chemical designed to produce a reversible chemical lobotomy. In other experiments, LSD was to be administered to unwitting victims in social situations through the use of bug bombs, swizzle sticks in drinks and a hypodermic needle that could shoot drugs into corked wine bottles. Some of the experiments' victims were men picked up in bars and brought to CIA safe house in San Francisco and New York by CIA-employed prostitutes who secretly administered the drugs.

Many of the MK ULTRA victims—the total number could run into the thousands—may still be suffering from after-effects. Dr. Peter R. Breggin, a noted psychiatrist and leading advocate of mental patients' rights, says that it is vital not only to locate the victims of MK ULTRA experiments, but also to expose the psychiatrists who used their patients as human guinea pigs.

Breggin likens the psychiatrists who were involved in the MK ULTRA experiments to the doctors in Nazi Germany who experimented on human beings. Rather than giving the MK ULTRA psychiatrists anonymity, as has been the policy thus far, Breggin says they should be tried for crimes against humanity.

"The use of LSD, psychosurgery and electroshock in these experiments could have long-lasting, profound effects," Breggin says. "Electroshock, for example, could have resulted in brain damage. As for drugs, many people who have voluntarily taken LSD feel they have lifelong problems with flashbacks. For persons who were given LSD when they weren't prepared and didn't even know they were getting it, they could be experiencing these same kinds of problems and not even know why."

Joseph Forer, the veteran Washington, D.C., civil liberties lawyer, is currently representing a client who believes she may have been the unwitting victim of an MK ULTRA experiment. (Forer says his client desires anonymity at this time.) The lack of government follow-up on the MK

ULTRA victims, Forer says, represents "typical government callousness. It's appalling."

CIA Director Turner, in testimony last August 3 before a joint session of the Senate Select Committee on Intelligence and the Subcommittee on Health and Scientific Research of the Senate Committee on Human Resources, said the CIA was "working with the Attorney General" to try to locate MK ULTRA test subjects. On September 21, Turner again testified before the Subcommittee on Health and Scientific Research; and in even more specific language assured the senators that the CIA had made arrangements to notify human guinea pigs in the MK ULTRA tests. The job of locating them, he said, had been turned over to the Justice Department.

What Turner did not say was that not only had Justice not even located anyone involved in the tests, they weren't even looking.

Justice Department officials would not comment on Turner's testimony, but gave a far different picture to *Seven Days* of that agency's involvement in the MK ULTRA follow-up than that presented by Turner.

John Gavin, of the Justice Department's Office of Legal Counsel, said that the Department's only effort to date involved compiling a report for the CIA on a number of "legal, quasi-legal and policy questions" concerning such issues as whether the CIA would have authority itself to try to locate persons involved in the experiments. (The CIA charter, despite the agency's widespread illegal domestic spying in recent years, actually does prohibit CIA operations and investigations in the United States.) The Justice Department's report would go only to the CIA, and not to the Senate committees, Gavin said, "and what the CIA does with it is their business."

Asked about Turner's testimony that last summer there was a program within the Justice Department to locate persons involved in the experiments, Gavin said he did not wish to comment. Then he added: "You could say there is the beginning of a program to locate them." But the problem, he said, is that the CIA doesn't have any names of persons involved in the tests. Why not? Because most documents on MK ULTRA were destroyed in 1973 at the order of then-CIA Director Richard Helms.

A source on the Health and Scientific Research Subcommittee said that the subcommittee would probably give the CIA until early this year to provide the requested information. Then, if the CIA still fails to do what Turner promised last summer, the subcommittee might possibly get impatient enough to hold hearings to find out what's behind the delays and inaction.

John Hanrahan is co-author of Lost Frontier: The Marketing of Alaska *(N.Y.: W.W. Norton).*

28 February 24, 1978

16. The Royal Way

Another busy signal.

Jeffrey hung up the phone for the third time in a row. He was trying to get through to Jonathan. He hoped to say how sorry he was that Jonathan had lost the big fencing meet, and he also wanted to work out their hypnosis schedule. But either Jonathan hadn't returned, or the line was always busy.

Finally he gave up, went off to the parking lot and found the old car he owned now that he had his Institute job. He headed off toward Linda's little cottage. He was nervous about seeing her. He had just finished reading a book for Romance Literature by a French existentialist named André Malraux, called *The Royal Way*, which was about a young adventurer named Claude who went off to Cambodia, explored the jungles, had steamy love affairs and got trapped right in the middle of a head-hunter war. Jeffrey fantasized that he was in the middle of an adventure that was as exciting as Claude's, going to meet his lover in an exotic hideaway in a secluded and dangerous foreign country.

He smoothed down his hair with the palm of his hand as he turned onto Linda's street. His hair was approaching Beatle-length like Jonathan's. Early Beatles, anyway. No way was he ever going to let his hair keep growing to his shoulders like the style that the Fab Four had adopted now.

Getting out of his car, he started worrying that if he got too involved with Linda, she might expect him to marry her – and he certainly wasn't looking for any major commitments. He knew Hugh Hefner's Playboy Philosophy by the book and according to the impeccable doctrine, a lot of girls who acted sexually liberated tended to develop a very itchy fourth finger of their left hand after a while, eager to get a bachelor to the altar before he even stopped to realize that his Playboy lifestyle would be doomed forever.

He parked down the street a few houses away, so as not to give the neighbors the idea that he was a constant companion of Linda. As he walked up the sidewalk, he saw two men under a streetlight, one sort of tall, the other shorter and chubby. They were walking quickly towards him on the sidewalk. They came to a stop right in front of him so he had to stop too.

"We'd like a few words with you," the tall one said and flipped a badge right in his face. Jeffrey tried desperately to read what the badge said, but the man tucked it away with lightning speed before Jeffrey could make out anything. Two words flashed through Jeffrey's mind again and again as his heartbeat accelerated: Plainclothes cops.

Jeffrey stood there stunned. He was certain that Linda had marijuana inside her house. Were these guys from the State Narcotics Division?

"Are you, uhm, police?"

"You saw my badge," said the tall one. "Did it say police?"

"You pulled it back so fast I didn't even see it. Can I see it again?"

"No. But I'd be happy to read you your rights if that will make this more official."

"What?" Jeffrey's heart rate was accelerating by the second. "What's this about?"

"Don't play innocent with us, Jeffrey, and don't talk shit," said the short, chubby one in a somewhat high voice. Oh God, thought Jeffrey – they knew his name! "We know all about you," the chubby one continued, "but let's talk about your friend."

"Which friend?"

"I said don't talk shit with us," the short one repeated.

"Jonathan?"

"We'll start with him, yeah," said Shorty.

"He's not in trouble, is he?"

"You like that shithead, right?"

"Shithead? You mean Jonathan? Well, we work together, and he's my friend. C'mon – what is this all about?"

"You do know what treason is all about, don't you?"

"Treason?" Jeffrey's blood pressure at that moment would have aroused alarm from those in the medical professions.

"That's where someone like Jonathan participates in secret government research and then gives the data to the enemy."

"Jonathan would never do something like that."

"He already has – and you're definitely implicated."

"Me?" said Jeffrey, with a little squeak in his voice. "Implicated?" Jeffrey could already hear what his mother and father were going to say about this, when they realized he'd been arrested. They'd say, 'Hypnosis, Jeffrey, it all started with that Institute. You didn't listen to us, did you? You had to do things YOUR way.'

"But we might go easy on you," said the tall one. "We have a proposition for you."

"What kind of a proposition?" Jeffrey asked. His suspicions about these two were intensifying rapidly.

"Once a week, on Wednesday at eight a.m., you're going to call this number and leave a message. You're going to tell us if Jonathan is walking the straight line, or if he's leaking stuff about the Institute research to the press."

"Or TV," said the short one.

"Why would he do that?" Jeffrey asked.

"Because he's a pinko fucker, or at least leaning in that direction. And we want you to report on his friend Pok. He's a suspect, too."

Jeffrey took the business card he was handed. It said Society for the Investigation of Human Ecology. And there was an 800 number. No name.

"Human ecology? What is this? Are you guys really cops? Or are you a couple of fakes who are trying to steal Bernie's research – is that it? That's it, isn't it?"

"October 6, 1966," said the short and chubby one.

"October what?" Jeffrey stammered.

"October 6, 1966 – that's a date you'd better remember. That's when LSD went from being a Schedule I drug to being completely illegal for any purposes whatsoever. There's major danger with all this LSD proliferation everywhere, and all this Timothy Leary 'Turn On, Tune In, Drop Out' stuff. He's going to end up in prison for sure, that Leary asshole. And as for your buddies, those yellow chicken-liver acid-heads, you'd better watch out or you'll all be busted. And here's some more advice – keep our little meeting here quiet, even from the squeeze you're playing with in there. It didn't happen. You got that? Say you got it."

"I got it," said Jeffrey, but he didn't really get it at all.

"We know you smoked pot with Pok."

How the hell did they know that, wondered Jeffrey? Unless Jonathan's dorm room was bugged.

"If you want to stay out of jail, we'd better hear from you at that 800 number – leave a message every Wednesday at 8 a.m. Miss one Wednesday and your ass is kaput."

"But – but wait a minute – that's crazy – you can't expect me to –"

They were already walking away and didn't hear him. Jeffrey was trying to catch his breath. Was it all a joke? Why hadn't that guy actually let him read that badge? Maybe the badge was bullshit. So now he was supposed to believe that Jonathan was a spy? And he'd been ordered to discuss this with no one, including Linda? No way!

The instant Jeffrey knocked, the door opened.

"Hi, Jeffrey."

"Hi, Linda. Whew. You're looking sexy as usual."

"Thanks." All she had on was a fancy silk slip-over gown that was rather short. "But you look like you just saw a ghost," she said, looking closely at him.

"No, no ghost."

"What then?"

"Oh – nothing. Nothing."

As they went into her living room Jeffrey did his best to conquer his unease. He noticed she'd improved the interior decor since his last visit. The entire living room was covered with oriental wall hangings and there were psychedelic pictures and posters everywhere.

"Do you like it?" she said. She pointed to a poster that showed two people actively involved in sexual intercourse in a weird convoluted position on top of a rock – that must hurt a naked butt, Jeffrey thought.

"It's, uhm, very nice," said Jeffrey. "Provocative."

"Take off your coat and make yourself at home, I was just mixing. Rum and Coke okay?"

"Just a Coke will be fine."

"Nobody could ever accuse you of being a lush."

"I got really drunk once back in high school. I had about six beers in one afternoon. My bladder hurt for a week."

"Sure you won't just try some rum? It'll make you feel nice and warm."

"Okay, if you insist."

She went over to prepare the drinks.

"Can I ask you a really frank question?" he asked.

"Go on, try me."

"Do you still have the hots for Matt?"

"No more than I do for any good old friend."

"It sure didn't exactly seem that way at Mike's party."

"Jeffrey, I think you're jealous. Are you?"

"Not exactly, but – well, why did you kiss him like that in front of me? Did you want me to see you?"

"That kiss had nothing to do with my feelings for you. It only had to do with my feelings for Matt."

"So do you want me to stop calling you and coming over, so you can be with him?"

"Tell me, does everything in life have to be either-or?" she asked, getting a little impatient with him.

"In relationships that's maybe just the way it is," he said.

"Only if you make it that way. When you've worked at the Institute a little more, you'll understand. We all should be able to express love for whomever we want. I shouldn't have to lock up my positive feelings just for one person, I have positive feelings for others too – sexual inhibition is a sickness of our society. Two positives don't make a negative."

"That's the philosophy of free love."

"Nothing in life comes free, Jeffrey. If we want to grow and express ourselves emotionally, we have to work at it, no matter who we happen to be with at any particular moment. Come on, let's enjoy our moment right now – this is what life is all about."

He shrugged his shoulders, took off his boots and then they cozied up on the thick rug sipping their drinks. Jeffrey had a look of disgust. He hated the taste of rum.

"Say, did I tell you I tried pot?" he said.

"Oh – did Jonathan turn you on?"

"Not exactly. It was one of his friends."

Now I've done it, thought Jeffrey. He'd mentioned his experience with pot to her, but he realized immediately that he'd promised not to take pot or any psychedelic drugs when he had become a subject. That is, he was not to take them unless he were given a micro-dose of LSD in conjunction with one of the hypnosis sessions under laboratory controlled conditions.

"Which of Jonathan's friends turned you on?" she asked.

"With pot? Uhm, it was Pok."

"Ah, I know Pok. Wow. Some guy. He was a subject for almost two years."

"Did you know that he was in jail in Morocco once?"

"Last time I heard, it was Afghanistan," she said. "And the time before that it was Tibet. So what did you think of smoking grass?"

"Well it was wild but I'm not going to smoke it again," said Jeffrey. "I just found out they have it classified as a narcotic in New Jersey, exactly the same as heroin. You can get sent to jail for around twenty years if they catch you. If I'd been arrested, I'd be getting out of prison when I'm about forty. What would my family say?"

"Yes, what would they say?" Linda repeated in a slightly sarcastic tone of voice.

"I mean, forty – that's too old to start medical school, don't you think? Plus the fact that having a felony on my record would probably disqualify me from getting a license to practice medicine."

"So then don't practice medicine. If they let you out of maximum security prison at age forty that isn't too old to start a career as a film director is it? There's a lot of ex-cons in Hollywood working in the movies and TV, aren't there?"

"I don't know," he said. "Is that true?"

"Of course it's true. And besides," she said lightly, "you might get a year or two knocked off for good behavior, you're such a nice boy. How do you like the drink?"

"Terrific," he lied. He was having trouble with every gulp. "Really, uh, hits the spot."

"I thought you'd like it. It's one of Jonathan's favorite drinks, or at least used to be."

"Say, have you noticed how different Jonathan's been acting lately?" Jeffrey asked her, voicing his concern.

"That's nothing new. Jonathan's always different."

"No, I mean *really* different."

"I did up an astrological chart on him," she said. "His planets are in really weird alignment right now."

"Can I tell you something in complete confidence?"

"Confide away."

"You won't breathe a word to Bernie or Jonathan?"

"My lips are sealed."

Uh oh, he thought. Was he really going to do it? Was he going to tell her about the two men who'd threatened him?

He reached into his pocket for the business card that had the phone number he was supposed to call on Wednesday. And then he panicked. The card wasn't there. He started frantically reaching from one pocket to another. The card was definitely gone. What would happen to him if he didn't make those calls?

"What are you looking for?" she asked.

"Two guys hassled me. It happened when I was on my way up to your place, so maybe they're staking you out or something. They gave me a mysterious business card about human ecology or something and demanded I spy on Jonathan and Pok and call them. I must have dropped it."

"Was that the Society for the Investigation of Human Ecology?" she asked.

"Yeah, that was it, how did you know that?"

"Don't pay any attention to those bastards," said Linda. "They have no authority to threaten you. They don't even have the right to interrogate people within the continental U.S."

"Who are they? Were they from the CIA or something?"

"They're part of what Bernie likes to call the Rogue Oversight Committee. You see, not all of our money comes from the National Institutes of Mental Health or N.I.H. Some of it is channeled through various organizations, and the human ecology group is one of them. That's where national security comes in. Believe me, they're not nice people, and they sometimes interfere and try to check up on things – like whether we're giving the hypnotic subjects drugs."

"I can't find their business card. I must have dropped it outside. They're going to make big trouble for me if I don't call them like they asked."

"Ignore them."

"I don't know if I can just ignore them," said Jeffrey. "They threatened me."

"It's just normal harassment."

"Normal? What's normal about it? And there's another thing on my mind. Jonathan told me he thinks the hypnosis experiments could mess me up."

"Oh? What does he say they could do to you?"

"Confuse me. Or it could cause flashbacks like they say LSD sometimes does. Screw up my memory like it did to him."

"Well Jonathan's just screwed up naturally, it goes with the territory, he's from a cattle ranch and cowboys are weird by definition. Out there all alone in love with their favorite horse, you know what I mean. Bernie went out on a limb to accept him as a subject in the first place."

"But Jonathan seemed really serious."

"When you really get to know Jonathan, if you ever do, you'll understand that he always believes what he says but half of it comes from his interior fantasies, and the other half of what he says is mainly for dramatic effect – whatever pops into his head at the moment. I still can't figure out why Bernie let Jonathan become a hypnotist. A hypnotist has to be sensitive and mature with a strong sense of responsibility."

"But Jonathan feels responsible for what might happen to me," Jeffrey protested.

"Seriously – don't let Jonathan's negative attitude screw up your own experience with the research. You're interested in psychology. You'll have a great future if you stick with Bernie."

Jeffrey was feeling giddy from his four sips of rum. "You're probably right," he agreed. "And I really do want to be a psychiatrist. At least I think I do. Most of the time. Then again, there are other times –"

"Shshsh, you're talking too much," she said. Linda snuggled closer to him, reaching up and stroking his hair. He felt a shiver of pleasure rush up from his balls to his brain and then he started stroking her hair too. "It's nice that you tell me your feelings about Jonathan," she said. "I'm glad you trust me. Hey, I've got a great idea, how would you like to take a bath?"

"What for? I showered this morning."

"No, I mean both of us."

"Really? You mean the two of us? Together?"

"Sure, it'll help you relax. C'mon, don't be shy."

In the bathroom Linda lit two candles and a stick of incense, turned off the overhead light and started filling the tub. She helped him unbutton his shirt and his belt and then without any warning at all dropped her gown from her shoulders and let it slip away from her body, causing Jeffrey to suddenly think of Claude in *The Royal Way* making love in thatched huts in the jungle while cannibals lurked outside in the shadows.

If only André Malraux could see him now!

17. Swallowing Time

Pok had been urging Jeffrey to try one of Pok's LSD sugar cubes ever since the night Jeffrey had first smoked pot. Pok regularly sang praises to LSD, claiming that it was the ultimate cure for the sickness of modern civilization – the ultimate cure for everything in fact – even the fear of death. To hear Pok explain it, taking LSD was like dying a temporary death of the ego. When Jeffrey had pressed him to explain what that meant, Pok had said: "Hey, it's not explainable – we're talking about the ineffable, about the subtle force of intelligence that lies behind all existence. How can you put any name on that at all, except nirvana?"

While watching Pok play pool one afternoon when Jonathan was off somewhere with Anne, Jeffrey listened to him describe his latest LSD trip which Pok said had blown him past all reality, he was now entirely free -- no longer needing to play any of society's games at all, and particularly not Princeton's pseudo-aristocratic Ivy League games. Not that he had done much Ivy League game-playing before that trip, he added – but now he had stopped turning in class assignments, and furthermore he refused even to worry about it.

"Worry is the biggest waste of time ever invented by man," Pok stated while chalking his tip. "It's future-based and the future, even time itself, is just one big illusion," he explained. "A prof might give me a bad grade on a paper just because it's late, but like the bard himself said, 'Life is a tale told by an idiot, full of sound and fury, signifying nothing.'"

Pok surveyed the lay of the colored balls on the table, aimed and fired. "On LSD," he continued while deciding on his next shot, "things become clear beyond all the sound and fury, the deepest levels of perception into life itself open up. So what are you waiting for, man?" he said, pausing to stare at Jeffrey through his World War I pilot goggles. "I offered to guide you on your first trip – what do you have against experiencing nirvana?"

"I'm excited about taking an LSD trip, I really am," said Jeffrey, "but I'm also worried about it being illegal."

"That's no excuse," said Pok. "Just repeat the pledge after me: 'I will not let the retrograde laws of the United States of America stunt my spiritual development.' Come on, now."

"Pok, I'm serious. And besides, I'm not sure I know what you mean by nirvana."

"Nirvana – the ultimate mode of consciousness, merging with the Non-self, experiencing infinite being-ness. It's total awareness of all things here and all things to come."

"Well sure, I really want to experience that, I really do. But you know it's against formal Institute rules for a subject to take any psychedelic. I mean, pot's one thing, but LSD is in a different category, isn't it? And I don't want to mess up the research data."

"Hey, how is one little acid trip going to mess up their research? And I told I'd be your guide, I can absolutely ensure you a most beautiful flight path."

At Pok's urging, Jeffrey had read a book by Timothy Leary and Richard Alpert called *The Psychedelic Experience: A Manual Based on the Tibetan Book of the Dead.* The book, which was all about taking LSD, had emphasized how 'set and setting' were essential for having a productive LSD experience: set meant your psychological state of mind at the time, and setting referred to your physical surroundings during the psychedelic experience.

Jeffrey had first become curious about the effects of LSD when major magazines like LIFE and LOOK had touted the fact that the famous actor Cary Grant had undergone LSD psychotherapy numerous times – and Cary Grant had praised the results. Meanwhile Timothy Leary had left Harvard and was living up at some extraordinary estate in Millbrook, New York, running something called the League for Spiritual Discovery and urging everyone alive on the planet to take LSD at least once. A recent interview with Timothy Leary in Playboy, in which he'd described the multitude of heavenly ecstasies that were part of the LSD experience, had a profound influence on Jeffrey.

And now finally, Jeffrey had reached the point where he said yes to Pok. On Sunday when Jeffrey's roommate was off-campus, Pok came over to Jeffrey's room with a sugar cube in his Levi's jacket pocket with a tiny dab of purple on it.

"This is only a hundred micrograms," said Pok. "A true beginner's dose - plenty to open the heavenly gates without blowing your mind completely."

Jeffrey held the cube in his left hand, stared it down – and then before he could even let negative images of parental disapproval flood his consciousness, he popped it into his mouth, crunched it between his teeth and washed it down with a glass of water.

"So how long does it take to start?" he asked.

"About half an hour," said Pok. "You'll start to tingle by then. Even a small dose comes on pretty strong when it hits."

Jeffrey had no idea what to expect – but sure enough, in about half an hour he discovered with an inner jolt that the experience was hardly anything like smoking pot. The changes beginning in his consciousness were subtle at first, and mainly visual. His roommate had a potted plant that Jeffrey hardly ever paid any attention to at all. Suddenly he noticed that the plant was sitting quietly there beside him in a somehow very commanding way. The colors on the ceramic pot were becoming brighter now, and louder, demanding that they be noticed. And the plant itself suddenly struck him as very much alive, in a luminescent way that he'd never noticed before. Each leaf in fact seemed to have its own expression, its own state of mind, its own reason for being alive right then in a room suddenly exploding with bright colors and strange shapes and swirling dancers emerging out of nothing ...

Jeffrey had of course also read Aldous Huxley's *The Doors of Perception*, about Huxley's first mescaline experience. Mescaline, he'd learned, was the main psychoactive ingredient of peyote, which certain native Americans were known to ingest to induce deep religious experiences. In fact, Jeffrey had been told that Dr. Osmond himself had been Aldous Huxley's guide.

Without warning all those convoluted thoughts vanished before his eyes as his ears woke up into a crystal-clear auditory brilliance. In fact everything in the room had now become bright and distinct, along with the plant and its pot. His eyes moved on their own around the room, and every object seemed to declare "I am!" in a joyous though entirely silent voice.

Pok met his eyes and just slightly smiled his Pokkian smile – and Jeffrey's heart in response seemed to explode outward in all directions at once with love. No words came to his mind or his mouth when Pok offered to put on some music. An album by Simon and Garfunkle called 'The Sound of Silence' started spinning around and around. When the music began, Jeffrey was overcome with emotion, as though hearing music for the very first time. The music blended with the colors of whatever his eyes took in, and the music seemed to become the colors and the colors became the music – everything merged together, including Jeffrey himself ... merging with absolutely everything in his surroundings.

"Enjoying your trip?" Pok asked.

"Trip," said Jeffrey. "Trippety Trippety trip. Hey. I'm on a trip." The word trip sounded strange, but then the meaning of the word leaped into his consciousness and he realized indeed he was on a trip, he no longer felt himself to be where he had been before. He could tell he was still in his dormitory room, but on some level he felt he had flown away, journeyed far into a whole new world where everything he gazed into was full of meaning and intention. He lost all sense of the past or future. He had traveled a very long way without even leaving his chair.

Suddenly his own existence itself, his own immensity, seemed terrifyingly gigantic, without form or purpose or inner center. And he found himself overwhelmed with fear because of a vast question that kept running back and forth through his mind. Even his mind itself no longer seemed to be intact, it changed and moved its location every split second. Every instant became a journey into a new unknown universe of color and music and feelings.

The question assaulting his mind was this: "Why is there something rather than nothing?"

The question plagued him, it gnawed at him from every angle and bothered him immensely. "Why should there be anything at all?" he said to Pok. "Why does any of all this even exist?"

"Ah, the eternal existential dilemma," said Pok with a grin. But that didn't explain anything. It left Jeffrey in a state of chaos, and the growing panic behind all the joyful feelings he'd been having seemed to expand until he felt convinced he was in fact entirely lost in some infinite limbo zone – but it was changing into a most beautiful limbo pulsating with joyful color, with everything melting into a gigantic kaleidoscopic image ...

He closed his eyes, opened them – and now he couldn't tell the difference between inside and outside. And somewhere, even though he now felt pleasant and relaxed once again, he was bothered about the fact that simple physical objects like the pot the plant was in, and human beings like himself and Pok, existed simultaneously side by side without any boundaries at all – and that plant never moved from its small bit of soil in its pot. What a boring, meaningless existence, having roots stuck in soil and never moving, never going anywhere.

Everything in his day-to-day habits suddenly became small and not real, of no consequence at all. He could see himself in his mind's eye, studying every day – and for what? For good grades? To get into medical school one day? Would he really go to medical school, study to become a psychiatrist? A psychiatrist, someone who was supposed to understand human beings, who could treat diseases of the mind. But wasn't even the normal state of the mind, with all of its anxieties and confusions and illusions, a diseased state of mind? His own normal state of existence didn't include all these new vast overwhelming feelings of joy – joy suddenly exploding because he now felt that he simply existed, joy that he could see and hear all this, joy just because he could inhale this air all around him …

He laughed outright at the realization that no course in philosophy or study of psychiatry would ever equal this ultimate feeling of really experiencing and knowing life. Pok seemed now to be a funny little gnome or angel who was on the verge of laughing outright along with him, as if they were one mind, one great eternal guffaw of the universe laughing at itself, with itself, to itself ...

Then everything became utterly calm, entirely clear. He understood perfectly clearly that he understood nothing at all. There was in fact, and this was the gigantic celestial joke, nothing to understand because everything in existence simply is – it all exists together simultaneously and someday none of it will exist. At the same time he suddenly felt to the depths of his heart and soul that something had in fact created him, had created everything in this room, had willed into existence everything on this planet, this solar system and onward into the great infinity of planets and space and stars. He could tell that the 'something' which had created all of this was hidden behind a veil, never to be witnessed directly, only sensed through the things that were its infinite creation ... and that was enough.

Pok led him on a walk outside. Jeffrey felt overwhelmed at the sight of each tree, every leaf and every single insect that scampered along tree bark or on the sidewalk. At one point being near the trees and insects became intensely repulsive. But then some creative switch was turned on inside his mind, new channels opened and he gained access to even more remarkable realms of thought and imagination. He was not Jeffrey anymore. He was not anyone or anything. He was simply a part of everything he saw, and he felt overwhelmed by every feeling of beauty and wonder and awe.

Time stretched out. It seemed like hours and days had gone by since he and Pok began walking, even though it had been less than an hour. It seemed as though they had walked for miles outside the dormitory, but in actuality, they had barely walked two hundred feet before turning around and returning to the dorm room.

About eight hours after ingesting the sugar cube, as the LSD gradually wore off Jeffrey felt he was losing something precious. He had entered another world, or rather many different worlds, while all the while remaining right here. Those other worlds seemed profound and beautiful and glorious, but strange – strange because they contained such a variety of things the mind would usually never imagine, and strange because existence seemed to joyously proclaim itself to be a great miracle.

A feeling of the ordinary was creeping back into his mind. A feeling of being Jeffrey again slowly took over. The colors were no longer so pronounced, the music not nearly so angelic. And then with a great sigh, he realized he was almost all the way back inside his own ordinary mind. An eternity had passed through him, even though in actuality, it had only been eight hours before the trip began to peter out and then came to a muffled, crashing conclusion.

Yes, he had entered the timeless realm of infinite energy beyond all time and space. As Aldous Huxley and Timothy Leary had promised, as Humphry Osmond and even Jonathan and Pok had loudly hinted: LSD would wash away all the dust and dross that clouded his everyday consciousness. He had seen the miracle of existence – but alas, the joy that had so suddenly and rapidly begun had now faded. He was back in his normal state, just sitting there in his chair. Everything was again quite ordinary – pitifully and sadly ordinary.

However, the next morning he still felt the effects of his psychedelic trip – he definitely felt lighter in his breathing, free of some invisible chains that had always been holding him back. He knew he'd continue with his pre-med program, but something had sprung to life deep inside him that was not compatible with a future career as a psychiatrist.

Another change that he noticed was that the hypnosis experiences out at the Institute became even more intense, more profound. He noticed it the day he reclined in the hypnosis chair in Bernie's office on a Monday morning. Jonathan hadn't shown up on time for their session, so Jeffrey gained an opportunity to work directly with Dr. Aaronson as his hypnotist for the first time.

"... and now imagine that you are lying on your back on a padded little raft, floating peacefully down a gentle river," said Bernie. "You can feel the warmth of the sun ... and you feel entirely calm, the world all around you is calm ... and now you are beginning to feel a light airy sensation in your right hand. Your muscles are totally relaxed, and as your hand fills with light weightless air, your hand begins to rise upward."

Sure enough, Jeffrey's arm was rising.

"Now touch your hand to your forehead. Feel it transfer its lightness to your head. Do you feel it?"

"Yes."

"Now the feeling is moving down through your chest, through your belly ... and it feels very good. Allow this wonderful weightless feeling to move down and fill your whole body at once."

Jeffrey could feel the air around him cushioning him, raising him up, letting him float off on a soft safe cloud.

"And now, when you hear your induction word, you will immediately fall into a very deep trance, a deeper trance than you have ever experienced. Are you ready?"

A moment of silence.

"Yes."

"Kambastena-mondora."

And indeed, Jeffrey fell. The trance deepened. He was floating in darkness. His mind was fading. Gone.

"I want you to focus on the sounds around you," Bernie's voice continued. "Concentrate on the highest-pitch sound you hear right now."

Scrapes and rubs and creaks. A hot water pipe, squealing, getting louder, so loud he could hardly stand it. He pressed himself against the back of the chair, tensing.

"It's hurting my ears."

"The pain in your ears is now going away. It's getting softer now, in fact the noises are becoming so quiet that the only sound you hear is my voice."

There was silence. Perfect silence. The trance deepened. Jeffrey was floating in deep bliss. Mind fading. Gone.

"I will now count from one to twenty, and at twenty, you will be even deeper – so deep that you will have no recollection of where you are, until I tell you. You will sense yourself surrounded by a thick, white fog, and that is all. One … two ... three ..."

Every single number was a powerful magnet. Pulling him to places he had never been before. Deep into the very center of the white fog.

"... eighteen ... nineteen ... twenty. You have arrived at the deepest level of the trance. Do you know where you are?"

"Yes. I'm in the fog," he said.

"Do you know where the fog is?"

"No."

"Look into the fog. You see a rope. Hang on to it."

"I'm going to fall from the clouds."

"You won't. The rope will hold you up. Hold on."

"I'm holding."

Jeffrey's hands were raised, clenched. Holding the rope. Invisible rope.

No, this was not like LSD, which had shown him reality with greater intensity. There was nothing real about what he was undergoing now. It was a false reality existing only in his mind, but it certainly did seem to him, in every sense, as if it were actually real.

"We're above the ocean. Now you can hear the sea. Do you hear it?"

"Yes."

The sea was pounding. Thunder was rumbling through his head, crashing on the ocean between his ears. There were great waves. His mind was liquid. His mind was the sea. Salt. Fish. Drowning.

"Swish the spit in your mouth."

Jeffrey swished. It was foam. Ocean foam, the tide was lapping at the beach of his brain.

"Swallow."

Jeffrey swallowed. It was the whole ocean. Pouring down his mouth, going down into his gullet, the sea forming inside of him.

"Do you see the ocean?"

"I swallowed it. The ocean is inside me."

"You are part of the ocean?"

"I'm the same as the ocean."

"You swallowed more than the ocean. Do you know what else you swallowed?"

"No."

"You swallowed time. Time is now inside you. Can you feel it?"

"Yes. I have swallowed time."

Jeffrey felt that time only existed inside him now. Time would progress for him, he would get older – in fact, someday he would grow very old and die. But time only existed inside him. There was no longer any time in the rest of the world.

"Now when you open your eyes in a moment, you will know that you are in a room, but you won't recognize where you are. You may open your eyes."

Jeffrey opened his eyes and blinked.

"You don't recognize where you are, do you?"

"Uhm – no."

"Notice that with every inhale, you're swallowing time ... you inhale again, you swallow more time and suddenly time has vanished from the outside world, but time is inside you. Eternal time. Always here ... just breathe effortlessly ... enjoy this eternal moment ..."

"Eternal time," said Jeffrey.

"So ... now you can close your eyes again. Good. And just let go entirely of who you are, and of where you are. Who you are is quietly vanishing, disappearing into the thick soft fog. You don't need to have a name anymore, you are simply a body and a brain. Everything you ever knew or thought about yourself, this is all vanishing... and as you breathe, time is slowing down, more and more, slower and slower ..."

Jeffrey was swallowed by the fog, lost in forever. Only his two eyes were left, still looking behind his closed lids, but seeing nothing in the darkness –

"We have gone beyond names now ... we have gone beyond egos ... we have gone beyond time. You feel completely secure here, in my loving presence, knowing that I have full power to protect you, knowing that no one else will ever know what we do here, we are behind a locked door and safe."

18. Happy Hunting Ground

Anne had packed a bag to go into New York for the weekend. A girlfriend from San Francisco had come east to the Big Apple for a job interview, and Anne wanted to see her. Jonathan walked with Anne up to Nassau Street, passing old and ornate Alexander Hall on the way to the great iron gates in front of the University. An early moon was full and low in the sky, and the wind was blowing, clouds soaring by overhead. The feeling of snow was in the air.

It seemed strange to Jonathan that it still hadn't snowed, the very best thing about Princeton was the first snowfall. Glen, Wayne and Rick thought Jonathan was nuts because he always ran outside and jumped and rolled around like a little kid when the first snowfall came. He felt a memory surging to the surface – one of the few fond remembrances of his youth that hypnosis somehow hadn't managed to erase. He remembered his mom coming and waking him up in the middle of the night so that he could watch the first snowfall of winter as it happened, rather than just wake up to its whiteness the next morning. His mom had been good about things like that. She had been good about a lot of things.

After Anne boarded the Greyhound for New York, Jonathan stood watching the smoky bus roar away down the usual early evening traffic of Nassau Street. He could feel his heart still somehow with her, he could almost feel himself sitting right there with Anne in the bus seat.

A flash of realization hit him – the feelings he was experiencing for Anne right then were almost exactly the same deep heart feelings he'd once felt for his mother, a very long time ago – and somehow that realization didn't seem weird to him at all right then. In fact it felt remarkably good. But then the moment vanished and he popped out of that momentary feeling. He remembered what he needed to deal with right then, and he went off fast looking for Pok, who'd failed to show up for dinner.

Pok wasn't in his room. Jonathan looked in the cafeteria and the pool room in the Student Center but Pok wasn't at any of his usual haunts. Jonathan even tried the soccer field. No Pok. There was one last spot he could be that was part of his natural habitat: the art room up in the tower of the Student Center.

Jonathan found the door that opened into the winding staircase and started climbing. When he finally reached the top of the stairs he could hear music – Ravel's 'Bolero.' The door to the art room was closed. Jonathan turned the doorknob, opened the door and walked inside. The room smelled of linseed oil and turpentine and something else slightly akin to grass. The circular space with its domed ceiling was dark except for the light of a single spotlight shining down on a spinning potter's wheel over in the far side of the room.

Jonathan closed the door. All he could see of Pok was the silhouette of his back hunched over a table. Holding a plastic squirt-bottle of paint in each hand, his body was swaying to the strong rhythmic pulse of the orchestral music while he squirted paint onto the spinning piece of paper on the table, poised like a matador ready to jab his swords into the neck of a charging bull.

'Bolero' has a hypnotic rhythm and a repeating melody that begins with the pianissimo voice of a single melodic flute and climaxes in ten minutes or so with full orchestra exploding into chaotic dissonance. It was, in Pok's interpretation, an almost perfect expression of the history of humankind. The music was now building to its climax and Pok was building to his, lost in time, squirting frantically.

Then the music was finished and fading into silence and Pok was spent – he sat down on the floor, his back still to Jonathan, an empty squirt bottle in each hand. The record player turned itself off with a loud click and then, after a long moment, Pok reached forward and switched off the spinning wheel. It slowed and slowed some more, and then the whirring faded into silence.

Pok spoke to the Void, his voice sounding depressed.

"Olé," he said. And then again, "Olé."

It seemed that he might just sit there forever. Jonathan was pretty sure Pok was tripping. He could sense it without a word passing between them. He wanted to tell Pok he was there, but Jonathan knew he'd scare Pok shitless if he so much as cleared his throat.

He watched as Pok reached into his backpack, took out his canteen and unscrewed the cap. Then Pok took a prescription bottle of pills out of his backpack and poured about twenty of them into his hand,

Pok sat there looking at the pills, then pulled down his goggles over his eyes, picked up the canteen with his other hand and got ready to pop the pills into his mouth.

"Hey, Pok," Jonathan said softly.

Pok jumped as if he'd been electrocuted.

"Sorry to scare you," Jonathan said, coming closer. Pok looked more depressed than ever before – depressed wasn't even the word for it. Crashed to say the least.

"What's happening?" Jonathan asked. "You look like the world just ended."

"Acutely close to the point."

"Are you tripping?" said Jonathan.

There was no answer for a moment.

"End of an era is all," Pok said finally.

"Was that a yes or a no?"

"Like I said, end of an era. They came."

"Who came?"

"You know who. Them."

"You mean your Space Brothers? When?"

"Just after dark."

It shook Jonathan up, the way Pok always insisted on the reality of visitations from Space Brothers. It would have been nice to see some evidence even just one time. But when people were tripping, like Pok obviously was right then, they didn't need evidence for anything their mind made into a reality for them.

"Where did you see them?"

"Down at the soccer field."

"What happened?"

"I was called upon, I heard them coming, I went down to meet them. They said I could come with them this time."

"You actually saw them?"

"Sort of."

"Sort of. So you're leaving the earth with them tonight?"

Pok looked at the pills in his hand. "They already left without me. We were all aboard their spaceship. They started their hyper-drive. We were all set to take off. But my backpack—"

"What about your backpack?"

"I'd forgotten my backpack. I couldn't leave without it. I ran fast all the way up to my room to get it and when I got back to the soccer field they were just ... gone. They'd left without me. So like I say, end of an era."

Suddenly Pok's expression snapped into trance, his head cocked and eyes blank. "Actually, you want to know the truth?

The real truth? They told me I couldn't come," he said, talking as if to himself. "They said I was an earthling and that I had to stay here and eat my karma shitcake like everyone else."

"Yeah, I guess that's the way it is—"

Pok stared a long time at nothing. Then he said, "Holy Mary, full of grass, blessed is the root of thy Tomb – Vesuvius napalmed, man, the holy spirit –"

"Hey, Pok, are you rushing on something?"

"Coming on strong."

"So let's go over to my room, listen to some music or something," Jonathan suggested.

"No – nowhere to go, nothing to do. Nada y pues ..."

"At least let me have those pills."

"I'm going to take them," said Pok.

"You know what'll happen?"

"I'll kick the bucket."

"You'll get your stomach pumped at McCosh Infirmary."

He gave Jonathan a long stare, saying nothing, and then he put the pills back into the pill bottle and tucked the bottle into a pocket.

Outside it was cold with trees swaying and shaking in the onslaught of the storm. They walked through the night with wind tearing at their jackets. The wild crazy strength of the night suited Jonathan's mood.

"Let's run," said Pok.

And so they ran all the way across campus – jumping low fences, sprinting across lawns, breathing hard and feeling their bodies rammed, battered and caressed by the wind. When they got to Little Hall they stopped outside to catch their breaths. Jonathan glanced at Pok – and Pok glanced back at him with a wild unbridled expression.

Up in Jonathan's room, Pok threw himself down onto the bed. Jonathan lit a candle and some incense. Pok said no to music. He moved, sat up and curled his legs into a half lotus. Jonathan sat beside him. A few minutes flowed silently by. Jonathan found himself realizing that the same compassionate feeling in his heart that he had had with his mom was also fully present in his heart for Pok.

Pok said: "Take a look at this."

He reached into a pocket and pulled out a letter. It was from Pok's girlfriend Shana. Sent from Mexico.

"Go ahead – read it," said Pok.

Shana was informing Pok in the letter that she didn't want him to come to her. She warned him that if he came to Mazatlan and found her, she'd split without telling him and head somewhere else. She had realized that Pok's personality had changed completely for the worse ever since he'd become involved at the Institute. She said he'd had a hypnotic lobotomy and she didn't know who he was anymore. He'd become too scary – end of story.

Jonathan put the letter down.

"It came this morning," said Pok.

"The letter?"

"No, that was yesterday. What came this morning was the realization that I've finally completely lost my cool – I've violated my own Pokkian Code."

"Well, the Chief has the power to change his Code."

"And I have," said Pok.

Pok stood up as if in slow motion and opened the window that overlooked the quad forty feet below. The cold air came rushing in. Jonathan took two steps toward him.

"Don't be stupid," Jonathan told him. "You're freaked out, remember?"

"Says who?" Pok stepped out onto the terrace.

"Says me."

Pok moved to the left on the small ledge, balancing precariously, his arms outstretched like a tightrope trapeze artist.

"Pok, come back, get off that ledge!"

"They won't bother to pump my stomach if I make that jump."

"You're not going to jump."

"I've always wondered about the Happy Hunting Ground. Time to find out if it really exists."

"Pok. Give me your hand. You could slip."

"You forget my Indian blood, puchito. We're not clumsy like you whiny white bastards. The only way I'll –"

Suddenly one of Pok's feet slipped, he lost his balance and dangled with one moccasined foot precariously on the ledge and the other leg suspended in mid-air.

Jonathan lunged halfway out the window and grabbed him by the arm.

"Pull!" cried Pok. "Help me!"

Jonathan pulled with all his might, his heart throbbing in his throat, scared that his boots would slip and he'd lose his hold. Then an overpowering image filled his mind. 'Fly – fly away!' He saw himself turning into a dove, raising his wings and flying – but he also knew that if he let his arms become wings and raised them to the sky, Pok would fall.

'Fly, Jonathan!'

He held on and pulled with every bit of his strength. Pok tumbled back into the room. Jonathan closed the window. Pok sat on the bed.

"Jeez. Thanks," said Pok, his body shaking.

For a long moment, neither of them stirred. Then Pok spoke, his voice clear. "Shit, I tell you, we've got to split this scene. Something's trying to make me kill myself – you saw it. Let's just go get in the MG and boogie out of here forever."

"Where would you want to go?"

"Well – Mexico. You and me."

"I can't just drop everything and split for Mexico."

"Why not?"

"There's Anne. And school. What about your degree?"

"Fuck my degree."

"Shana doesn't want you to go to Mazatlan."

"Who's going to Mazatlan?"

"Pok, come on, get real."

"I'm as lucid as the Buddha. We could do Puerto Vallarta or maybe Cuernavaca."

"Pok, listen to me. I've got things to do right now tonight before I even think of anything else. That's why I was looking for you."

"Glad you were looking. I was right on the edge."

"You better now?"

"Yeah. I owe you one."

"Look at what I have here."

"So – what's that for?"

Jonathan was dangling a small key in front of Pok's nose. "This is a copy of the key to the file cabinet where Bernie keeps his secret files. Anne's hot, she made the copy for me. I'm going out there to finally find out what kind of shit's actually been coming down on us. I'll get your file too if you want."

Pok grinned his Pokkian grin. "Hey, bonanza man. And look at all that."

Jonathan turned and glanced out the window. It was snowing. "I thought it would never come."

"It's an omen."

"Listen, snow or no snow, I'm heading out to the Institute. Want to come?"

"Not possible. I'm totally spent."

"Will you stay here in my room till I'm back?"

"Sure. I'm feeling set to snooze."

"What about giving me those pills?"

"Hey, you can trust me. I'm all right."

"I'd feel better if you'd let me flush them."

"Well –what the hell," Pok agreed, handing them to Jonathan. "I'll bet the crocodiles could use a good buzz."

Justices Give CIA Sweeping Secrecy Powers

By PHILIP HAGER, *Times Staff Writer*

WASHINGTON—The Supreme Court ruled 7 to 2 Tuesday that the Central Intelligence Agency has sweeping authority to maintain the secrecy of its far-ranging sources of intelligence data.

The court said that, even when disclosure would not affect national security, the CIA may reject requests under the Freedom of Information Act for the names of scientists, researchers and others who provide intelligence or for the titles of the books, journals and other documents the agency analyzes.

Congress' Intent Cited

"Congress intended to give the director of central intelligence broad power to protect the secrecy and integrity of the intelligence process," Chief Justice Warren E. Burger wrote for the court. "The reasons are too obvious to call for enlarged discussion; without such protections, the agency would be virtually impotent."

The justices overturned a federal appeals court ruling that said the CIA could withhold the identities of only those sources who provided information that could not be obtained without guaranteeing confidentiality. They said that the forced disclosure of any intelligence source could have a "devastating impact" on the agency.

Dissent by Marshall

Two justices, although agreeing in a concurring opinion that the appellate ruling had been too restrictive, argued that the Supreme Court had gone too far.

Justice Thurgood Marshall, joined by Justice William J. Brennan Jr., said that the justices' broad grant of authority to the CIA will "mangle, seriously," congressional efforts to balance the public's interest in obtaining information with the government's need for secrecy.

The decision was also denounced by a lawyer representing a group that had sought the names of private researchers and institutions

Please see CIA, Page 10

continuation:

Los Angeles Times

CIA: Court Holds Agency Has Sweeping Secrecy Powers

Continued from Page 1

involved in a controversial CIA drug experiment begun in the 1950s.

"This comes close to being a complete exemption of the CIA from the Freedom of Information Act," said Paul Alan Levy of the Public Citizen Litigation Group of Washington. "It is a severe setback for the public's right to learn about abuses by national security agencies."

Levy said that the ruling would enable the CIA and, perhaps, other intelligence-gathering agencies, not only to refuse to disclose sources of information but to "hide the details of almost any program that it would prefer the public not know about—so long as it claims (that) disclosure of the information might lead to disclosure of the persons who provided it."

The ruling was issued in a case (CIA vs. Sims, 83-1075) involving an attempt by the Ralph Nader Public Citizen Health Research Group to obtain the names of 185 college professors and other researchers and 80 institutions that participated in a CIA project involving mind-altering drugs. The government said that the program [illegible] counteract Soviet and Chinese advances in brainwashing and interrogation techniques.

In some aspects of the project, researchers surreptitiously administered drugs to unwilling subjects—a practice the government now forbids. The Nader organization said that it wanted to get more information to see whether researchers fully knew what the project involved and whether persons who were harmed by it had grounds for a lawsuit.

59 Institutions Named

The agency provided the names of 59 institutions that consented to disclosure, but it refused to release the names of the researchers or the remainder of the institutions. The dispute went to court in 1978.

The Freedom of Information Act calls for broad disclosure of government records. But Congress has also provided several exceptions to allow officials to keep some information secret. One such exception protects classified national defense and foreign policy information. The CIA relied on another, which gives the agency's director the responsibility for "protecting intelligence sources and methods from unauthorized disclosure."

The court, in its ruling Tuesday, concluded that the CIA director had free rein to define the "intelligence sources" that the agency needs to protect. The justices reviewed the legislative history of the agency's creation in 1947 and its congressional mandate to gather and evaluate intelligence from sources ranging from businessmen who travel abroad to technical and scientific reports.

If potentially valuable intelligence sources think that the agency may not be able to guarantee confidentiality, they may refuse to provide information, the court noted. "Even a small chance that some court will order disclosure of a source's identity could well impair intelligence gathering and cause sources to 'close up like a clam,'" Burger wrote.

19. The Night the Bogeyman Died

The MG didn't start the first three tries. When Jonathan looked up through the windscreen into the snow, under a lamp post he saw two men coming toward him walking fast. They had on suits and although he couldn't see their faces, he was sure he recognized them – the two spooks who'd threatened him. Had Bernie found out someone had copied that key that he had in his pocket? But then he wasn't sure. Maybe it was just two professors, or two grad students.

On the fourth try, the MG started up. Cold air whistled through the cracks of the fabric top as Jonathan popped the clutch, spun wheels in the two inches of snow, did a doughnut and roared off in the opposite direction, taking the back exit out of the parking lot. The snow was coming down harder now but he kept up max speed until a Volkswagen bug came around a corner and they almost smashed into each other. Jonathan swerved, going way too fast, and slid sideways across the snow-covered road, coming to a stop facing the wrong direction. He sat there a moment, stunned. Then the sound of another car coming toward him brought him to life.

The night guard at the Institute gate knew him and let him in. And the night watchman at the main door of the building, a tall tough guy with his pistol worn prominently on his hip, acquiesced when Jonathan explained he was expecting a subject for an evening session. He went on up the stairs, walking softly to keep his boots from clattering in the hallway.

Jonathan opened the door to Bernie's office and scanned the room. There was nobody inside. He could hear the hum of

EEG equipment from down the hall. Bernie was probably there, using the machine on a subject. There were some papers on top of Bernie's desk. Jonathan walked in, closed the door and thumbed through the pile – just some notes for a lecture Bernie was going to give somewhere, another smokescreen publicity gig to throw the public off his rotten scent, thought Jonathan.

He went over to the subject file cabinet. It opened smoothly when he inserted the key. Thanks Anne! The first thing he found was a folder filled with recent correspondence. He started reading a paper about possible uses of hypnosis for espionage missions – it referred to using operatives who were trained hypnotic subjects. These operatives, when committing clandestine operations like theft and assassinations, would be made to identify consciously with fictitious identities that had been created for them in hypnosis sessions. All memories of their personal lives would be entirely erased, they would have no sense of a past or future – only an eternal present. The perfect ruse.

And then he was reading quickly through a typewritten paper about an ongoing hypnosis program for employees who were being retired from active service. He read that the process had been proven – it actually could obliterate sensitive information permanently from consciousness, making the information totally irretrievable except through hypnotically-induced code signals. Again – several recommendations for applying this new hypnosis procedure out in the field with covert operatives.

With his heart pounding in his temples, Jonathan searched through two other cabinet drawers and suddenly located what he was after – Bernie's recent subject files. It seemed that subjects were identified by number only – what number was he? Glancing through the thick files one by one, he couldn't find anything that seemed to fit him or Pok. But he saw a folder marked Trance Induction Code. He scanned the list of code words and when he saw Callubra-Collorum he felt shivers run up and down his spine. The list said it was a phrase from James Joyce's book, *Finnegan's Wake*. His subject number was right there alongside the code-word – he was Subject #24.

His file was about two or three inches thick He pulled it out and tossed it onto Bernie's desk. How was he going to find Pok's file without knowing Pok's code-word? How much time had gone by, would Bernie be returning to his office, or maybe those two guys arriving out here? He raised his head and listened. He could hear the ticking of a strobe light coming from the EEG room. Bernie or somebody was definitely there, just down the hall.

Jonathan went through Bernie's outer office, stepped out into the hall and walked down three doors to the observation room with its one-way window into the EEG room. Sure enough, Bernie was sitting in there next to the machine – and there was Jeffrey in a reclining chair having his brain zapped. Jonathan noticed the electrodes glued to Jeffrey's head at the five hot spots – two on the forehead, two a little farther back, one down low toward the back of the neck. Jeffrey's eyes were closed and colored strobe lights were flashing onto his face. Jonathan watched Jeffrey's face glowing red and purple under the flickering of the strobes.

He left the observation room and went back into Bernie's inner office. There was one other cabinet to try – but when he opened and pulled out the file drawer, he found something entirely different – four quart bottles of pure Sandoz LSD. That was so much acid it was hard to contemplate. A mere one hundred micrograms was enough for an entry level trip. Four quarts? It was enough to get the whole city of New York plus half of New Jersey and Connecticut flying high alongside Lucy in the sky with diamonds.

He lifted one of the quart bottles out of the cabinet by its neck. Maybe he should bring it back to Pok as a birthday present, in honor of the fact that he was still alive. Or take it to the authorities and get Bernie permanently busted.

"Jonathan!"

He froze in his tracks and turned. There was Bernie standing just five feet behind him.

"What are you doing here?"

"I'm busting you – you and I both know that this acid was supposed to have been turned in when Lyndon Johnson closed the LSD part of Humphry's operation. Oh – and by the way, I'm quitting."

For a moment Bernie didn't reply. He walked over to Jonathan and held out his hands, implying that Jonathan should give him the bottle. Jonathan hesitated, then clutched the bottle more tightly.

"Jonathan, you must realize that you're not the only subject who's felt confusion – who's felt a wavering sense of purpose. That's only natural. But you must fully understand that we simply cannot let subjects walk away without giving them proper attention and help."

"I've had more help from you than I can handle," Jonathan muttered, feeling hard in his gut. "You've been messing with my life non-stop for the last year and a half, and now I've had my fill of you, deferment or no deferment."

"Yes, I can see this now. I've also been giving a lot of thought lately to your association with this Institute."

"Fuck you – you're screwing up innocent people's minds and emotions. I know you're doing something illegal, I just read some articles – I'm going to find some way to close you down."

Bernie suddenly glared at him with a tense, hostile look. "And I'm warning you," he said, almost growling. "If you try to undermine my research in any way by spreading rumors or whatever you have in mind, I'll have no choice but to present my records on your mental instability. You're suffering from serious psychotic delusions, Jonathan."

"Like I said – fuck you, I'm through."

"You most certainly are. In light of what you're saying, as of this moment I'm removing you from your position on our staff. You don't realize who you're dealing. Now you put that bottle down."

Jonathan stared hard at him for a tense moment of indecision, he saw his predicament in a flash – and still he felt a strong impulse to throw the Sandoz bottle of LSD at Bernie. But he managed to control himself, thinking mainly of Anne. He put the bottle down with a loud bang on the desk, pivoted on his boot heel and headed down the stairs, the sound of his boots echoing through the building.

He half-expected the watchman at the outside door to pull his gun and detain him, or maybe shoot him in the back as he stomped fast across the parking lot and got into his MG.

Then he was off and away.

Non-Drug Produced Altered States of Consciousness

The Production of Altered States of Awareness.
Supported by Erickson Educational Foundation Grant
Principal Investigator: Bernard S. Aaronson, Ph.D.

The interest in altered states of consciousness includes an interest in all methods that produce such awareness. The gift of an Altered States of Conciousness Induction Device by Mr. Reed Erickson has enabled us to study the phenomena of hypnagogic experience, the visions and sensations all of us experience as we go to sleep. The device is a platform suspended from a pivot which can be rocked either by an experimenter, or driven by the body's movements in breathing. At the present time we are gathering a series of records to ascertain the kinds of experience produced by exposure to this device.

A program on the effects of body massage is also being carried out. Studies in this area involve consideration of changes in self-concept, in attitudes towards others, in body image and in tension levels. The role of massage in enhancing interpersonal relationships is also being investigated.

A program studying the effects of sound stimuli delivered to various parts of the body is also being conducted. The focus of the study at the present time is on the nature of the experience. Experiences obtained have been compared by subjects to the effects of psychedelics, whether or not they themselves have ever experienced psychedelics and also, among those subjects engaging in meditation, to the effects of meditating constantly for four or five days.

20. Delusional Thinking of the Paranoid Kind

Jeffrey right away suspected something was askew when Bernie awoke him abruptly from his trance and unhooked the electrodes from his head. Jeffrey asked him if there were something wrong but Bernie just scowled, said they'd discuss it some other time, and he sent Jeffrey back to Princeton. As he hurried out, Jeffrey noticed that the security guard was upstairs looking around Bernie's outer office. Normally the guard stayed downstairs or in the kitchen.

The next day, Linda phoned Jeffrey and told him that there had been a serious security leak at the Institute, and that Jonathan was to blame. "I knew Jonathan was an expert at making shit hit the fan," said Linda, "but I never thought he'd have the nerve to break into Bernie's file cabinets."

"Jonathan did that?" Jeffrey reacted, dismayed. "Does this mean I won't be having sessions with Jonathan this week?"

"I think you've had your last session with the psychedelic cowboy," she retorted, her voice sounding cool and distant. "Bernie fired him."

"I don't believe it."

"Believe it, Darling – and Bernie wants you to get out to the Institute on the double."

As soon as Jeffrey arrived, Mike took him aside in an office on the second floor to ask him what he knew thus far about what'd happened with Jonathan.

"All I know is what I heard – that Jonathan broke into Bernie's office last night, and that he's been fired."

"It's worse than that. Jonathan's had a critical breakdown. It looks like it might be schizophrenia."

"But people don't just come down with schizophrenia from one day to the next."

"I'm telling you, Jonathan's mind completely cracked – a psychotic break. Bernie was with him when he went over the edge. You were here last night when it happened, but Bernie said you were out cold in a trance and didn't hear a thing."

A picture popped into Jeffrey's mind of Jonathan in a strait-jacket sitting in a psycho ward filled with dozens of pathological cases. "What hospital did they take him to?"

"It's not that kind of schizophrenic break," Mike explained. "He can still function, just barely – but if he doesn't get professional help they'll have to hang him out to dry in a sanitarium for a year or two – or even his whole life."

"What did he do, exactly – when he cracked?"

"He started making all kinds of totally irresponsible accusations about our research, right to Bernie's face. He even threatened Bernie. He told him that he was going to make up all kinds of outrageous lies about us and spread rumors to the press about Bernie illegally distributing LSD. Bernie didn't have any choice of course. He fired him on the spot."

"Maybe he just had a temporary mental explosion," said Jeffrey. "If I could get in touch with him and talk to him, I'll bet he and Bernie could patch things up again."

"Don't even think about it," Mike ordered. "Bernie fired Anne too, and the way things are now, if you try to interfere, it would be like sticking your neck into a spinning helicopter blade. Unless you'd get a kinky thrill out of being decapitated, I'd lay low if I were you."

"But – what caused Jonathan's breakdown?"

"We knew all along that Jonathan had a tendency toward schizophrenia, from his MMPI scores. And he also demonstrated a consistently anti-social attitude – he was obsessed with being independent and confrontational. But the main precipitating cause, in my opinion, was his tendency to get involved with psychologically unstable women – last spring it was a townie named Lucy. She didn't even have a high school diploma. There were rumors she was gang-banging Jonathan's friends, right while he was going steady with her. The only reason Bernie gave Anne a job was to keep tabs on her influence on Jonathan."

Jeffrey felt short of breath. His palms were sweaty. This was all coming at him too fast –

"But I have a very favorable impression of Anne," Jeffrey said.

Mike laughed a short amused cackle. "I noticed her little fetish action with you at my party that night. Didn't it strike you as odd, the way she kept fondling your hands?"

"No, I thought she was nice. She seems to really care about people."

Mike started filling his pipe with tobacco from his tin, pressing it down carefully with his pipe tool. "I don't mean to sound superior, Jeffrey – but you're obviously a bit naive, it goes with the territory because you're only a sophomore. Like Bernie says, Anne's a confused, disturbed, maladjusted runaway who's convinced herself she's an artiste – the very kind of concubine Jonathan likes to collect for his harem. That is, when he's not making time with his boyfriend Pok."

"What?" Jeffrey said – he couldn't possibly have heard what he thought he heard.

"You probably didn't know about that either. I hope I'm not shocking you."

"Come on, Mike, no way am I going to believe that about Pok and Jonathan."

"Well enough said then, I'll leave you with a few cherished illusions still intact – there's no point in shattering your entire world view."

Mike paused to light his pipe slowly and methodically, as though imitating Sherlock Holmes. "Pok had exactly the same problem with women," he went on. "His girl Shana – phony as a three dollar bill – the type of street girl who wanders into Princeton hoping to find a rich man to marry."

"But if Jonathan and Pok both developed serious problems, couldn't it have been caused at least partly by all the hypnotic conditions?"

Mike leaned over closer to Jeffrey and began talking in a very low voice even though the door was closed. "I'll tell you a secret. We never intended to let Jonathan do more than teach you how to get into a light trance. Bernie kept Jonathan around as a hypnotist so he could observe him. Bernie knew the day would come when he'd have to fire him. He should have done it sooner, but you know, Bernie is so soft-hearted. That's our boss, Jeffrey – just too nice a guy."

When Jeffrey was called into Bernie's office, the first thing Bernie did was hand Jeffrey an official Institute memo forbidding every staff member from having any further contact with Jonathan – either socially or professionally. It was an ultimatum. Anyone on the payroll who disobeyed would be fired.

"But he's been my friend," Jeffrey complained. "Is it true what Mike said, about Jonathan suddenly having a schizophrenic breakdown?"

"That's reasonably accurate. Jonathan is very seriously disturbed. He's in need of help and I hope he gets it. Unfortunately it's no longer possible for us to help him here. If you value being part of our team, honor my strict instructions not to see him. If he calls you, avoid him. And if he does make contact with you, keep it as brief as possible – and report back to me, is that clear?"

Jeffrey sighed, but nodded. He glanced down at his cowboy boots. He knew secretly that he would never have peace of mind until he had a chance at least to hear Jonathan's side of the story.

The very next afternoon he went over to Jonathan's room on the pretext of returning the book he'd borrowed on Tantric sexual yoga. The door opened and there he was.

"Oh, Jeffrey, come on in. How's things?"

"Oh, okay I guess. But I'm really going to miss our hypnosis sessions. I couldn't believe you got fired."

"Is that what they're saying at the Institute, that I was fired?"

"Isn't that what happened?"

"Hardly. I quit."

"Is it true that you, er, sort of cracked up?"

"Is Bernie saying that, too?"

"He says you've had a schizophrenic breakdown."

"I figured he'd start pulling stuff like that. Sorry to disappoint you, but I'm as lucid as Buddha, as Pok would say."

"Bernie told everyone at the Institute not to see you. I mean, I can get fired for just talking to you."

"So let him fire you. Get out while you still can."

"But I'm learning a lot from hypnosis."

"If you stay on as a subject, they'll bend your mind totally out of shape. They'll try to take you over completely."

There was a long silence.

"I'm sorry, Jonathan, but I want to be able to use hypnosis with patients when I'm a psychiatrist."

"Well then, you're going to learn the hard way, like Pok and I did."

"I'm confused, everything at the Institute seems really great to me – and yet you're fighting them."

"People gotta do what they gotta do. You don't know shit yet about the Institute."

"But have you turned against their research altogether?"

"Of course not. LSD is the most amazing consciousness tool ever discovered. But tools can be misused. They are being misused. As soon as the establishment realizes we've come up with something powerful for the good, something that can liberate people's minds from cultural programming, the establishment goes to work to subvert it, to use the tool to manipulate consciousness rather than liberate it – and I think that's a goddamn crime against humanity!"

There was an awkward moment of silence after Jonathan finished his diatribe. Then Jonathan said: "Hey, I have things to do – best of luck, Jeffrey. See you around sometime."

"Uhm, yeah, see you, Jonathan."

And that was that. The parting of the ways.

That night Jeffrey emotionally let go of his hypnotist – the cord was cut. He shifted into feeling positive knowing that Mike would be his hypnotist now. And Jeffrey packed up his cowboy boots and went back to wearing pointy black shoes.

21. Epilogue

Jonathan didn't get knocked off by CIA agents – but a few months later they came busting into Anne's apartment in Princeton when Jonathan was sleeping there – as near as Jonathan could tell, it was because he had talked again with President Goheen and had threatened to write a full disclosure on the Institute and its connection both to Princeton and the CIA. Apparently Jonathan's so-called 'guardian angels' had somehow received word of that meeting, thus the late-night visitation at Anne's apartment – which so scared the young couple that they panicked, packed up the MG and headed for the west coast.

Jonathan didn't wait around to graduate nor even take his final exams, but much to his surprise, when he needed his Princeton diploma to attend the seminary in San Francisco, President Goheen personally signed and sent him a diploma in good faith, which Jonathan much appreciated.

Jonathan didn't know it then, but a full disclosure of what was happening at the Institute would have been impossible at that time, and probably even today, because the full extent of all the MK-ULTRA facts will never be known.

It wasn't until ten years later, in 1977, when word first leaked in the press about MK-ULTRA, which was the code word for CIA mind control experimentation on American citizens. There were at least 149 projects related to mind control, of which the research at the New Jersey Neuro-Psychiatric Institute was only one such project. These projects took place at universities and hospitals and in other situations where unsuspecting people were lured into becoming guinea pigs. Millions of dollars were spent, with none of the funding issued directly by the CIA, but rather expended by dummy corporations that had been set up by the CIA, such as the Society for the Investigation of Human Ecology.

An attempted cover-up of all of this almost succeeded. It would have succeeded, in fact, if some unknown employee at the CIA in Langley, Virginia, hadn't mislabeled many boxes of files about MK-ULTRA as old financial records. Someone stumbled upon those boxes, and it became headline news for weeks.

There were Senate hearings in which then CIA-Director Stansfield Turner expressed shock over the fact that all of this had taken place during the tenure of one of his predecessors, Richard Helms. Senator Ted Kennedy made a speech about how this reflected a dark period in the CIA's history but had no relation whatsoever to the work of the CIA in 1977. Initial claims that MK-ULTRA terminated prior to 1968, when our story takes place, were proven to be false, and the facts on this were substantiated in the press and in research reported in books on MK-ULTRA.

The N. Y. Times reported on CIA MK-ULTRA projects connected to both Princeton University and Columbia University. One of the liaisons in the relationship of Princeton and the New Jersey Neuro-Psychiatric Institute was Dr. Carl Curt Pfeiffer, who was head of the Princeton Brain Bio Center, which was renamed the Carl C. Pfeiffer Institute after his death in 1988.

As for Dr. Bernie S. Aaronson, at some point after the MK-ULTRA revelations, he was dropped from the American Psychological Association, but he did continue to work as a private therapist in New Jersey specializing in 'Touch Therapy.' And as for Dr. Humphry Osmond, he soon departed from New Jersey after the MK-ULTRA exposure and ended up working at a psychiatric institute in Alabama. After Princeton, that was like heading for Siberia.

The New Jersey Neuro-Psychiatric Institute underwent a name change to the New Jersey Developmental Center – a name that suggested nothing whatsoever about its continued involvement in research and treatment of psychotic resident patients. The name change enabled the retiring of previous files. The Developmental Center had many security guards, and Jeffrey, while trying to look into the truth of these matters in 1988, was hassled by an armed guard for driving onto the grounds.

On July 1, 2014, the New Jersey Developmental Center, alias the New Jersey Neuro-Psychiatric Institute, shuttered its doors and its buildings were boarded up.

Jeffrey remained at the New Jersey Neuro-Psychiatric Institute after Jonathan's departure in 1968, and things did not go well with Mike as his hypnotist. Jeffrey finally came to many of the same realizations Jonathan had reached. He also suffered after-effects of the hypnotic conditions. After Jeffrey withdrew as a subject, Bernie offered to be his therapist – his 'private" psychotherapist' in a private office in Princeton, for which Jeffrey was to pay standard rates for Bernie's services. That relationship lasted only one session, in which Bernie attempted 'Touch Therapy' while Jeffrey was fully conscious, and Jeffrey simply freaked-out.

With his father as a noted professor at Georgetown University, Jeffrey sought additional psychological help at Georgetown University Hospital (to try to overcome the after-effects and flashbacks from the hypnotic conditions). He could not have known then (and certainly his parents did now know) that even Georgetown Hospital had participated in the CIA's MK-ULTRA research. That fact also made it into the newspapers during the exposé of MK-ULTRA in 1977.

Jonathan's fate after exiting the scene at both the Institute and Princeton took some fortuitous turns, thanks to the quite famous author of *Psychotherapy East and West.* When Jonathan and Anne arrived in San Francisco, Alan Watts put them up, and he got Jonathan a job during the summer of 1968 guiding Berkeley physics and math professors on 'creativity-enhancement' mescaline trips. Then Alan helped Jonathan land a draft-deferred graduate position at the San Francisco Theological Seminary where, sure enough, those same two 'guardian angel' spooks paid Jonathan two more visits just to let him know that he was still 'on their radar screen.'

Jonathan was not drafted, and neither was Jeffrey.

For several years Jonathan and Jeffrey had kept their distance from one another, having cut off communications after Jonathan departed the Institute in 1968. Then circumstances finally brought them back together three years later in 1971. Jonathan was still in California at the San Francisco Theological Seminary. Jeffrey, after successfully completing all his pre-med courses (including organic chemistry), suddenly dropped all plans to go to medical school to become a psychiatrist and decided he did have a destiny in Hollywood. His ultimate realization about his destiny came to him in an epiphany one night in London (while he was in Europe as a summer work abroad student in the summer of his junior year). It was the night he saw the premiere of The Beatles film "The Yellow Submarine." For Jeffrey, that was the wakeup call to put medical school behind him and devote himself to movies, animated and otherwise.

He was accepted as one of the first full fellowship students to attent the American Film Institute Center for Advanced Film Studies, which was located at the resplendent Doheny mansion in Beverly Hills.

Jonathan (who writes as John Selby) went on to become a therapist, entrepreneur, songwriter and published author of several dozen books. He remained with Anne (not her real name) for a time, but she was not destined to be his life partner.

Jeffrey (Paul Jeffrey Davids) went on to a career in writing, producing and directing films on many topics, including dramatic films and documentaries, most released to television worldwide by NBCUniversal International Television. The first feature he directed is called "Timothy Leary's Dead," a documentary biography which was begun about nine months before Timothy Leary's death in 1997. Dr. Leary authorized the film when he learned that Paul Jeffrey Davids had worked with Dr. Humphrey Osmond. Paul was thus still considered one of the 'psychedelic family.'

Paul Jeffrey Davids (left) directing Dr. Timothy Leary

"Timothy Leary's Dead," which is still widely seen today online, covers all aspects of Dr. Leary's life, including the various levels of heaven and hell Timothy Leary experienced. That includes his landing in prison for marijuana possession and escaping, and even hiding out with the Black Panthers in Morocco before being re-arrested in Afghanistan. The title comes from lyrics in a Moody Blues song called "Legend of a Mind."

That first wild rush up 'Psychedelic Hill,' as this true story documents, did result in many psychological casualties. Psychedelics are powerful and sometimes dangerous drugs. That's why Dr. Humphry Osmond proposed to Congress that the government and NIH set up officially licensed LSD therapy centers, so that responsible adults, under professional supervision, could experience mental states of psychedelic expanded consciousness without breaking the law. That never happened, of course – at least not yet.

To this day, the authors of this book still feel that in an enlightened society, consciousness explorers should be able to experience expanded consciousness in a safe set and setting under the care of trained LSD guides in an entirely legal context. The same should hold true of the use of other long recognized 'psychedelic vegetables' (as Timothy Leary used to say) – psilocybin ("magic mushrooms") and mescaline (peyote), which is actually legal as a sacred and holy sacrament for members of the Native American Church. It's just not legal for anybody else.

If potential explorers take tests that screen out unstable candidates, the whole process conceivably could reduce risks to a minimum, and the possible rewards (like those actor Cary Grant spoke of when he greatly benefitted from LSD psychotherapy back when it was legal) could be maximized.

Our human quest for self-awareness, for freedom of mind and soul, for psychic breathing space in which to discover who we really are, continues apace today. As slow as progress is, some of the steps forward have been noteworthy nevertheless. Dr. Timothy Leary was originally sentenced to ten years in prison for possession of one joint of marijuana. His 'crime' of marijuana possession resulted in his being incarcerated for a while in a cell in Folsom Prison next to the cell occupied by murderer Charles Manson.

Today marijuana use has been legalized in 29 States for medical purposes and is legal as a recreational drug in some of those by the choice of voters. The Federal government continues to list cannabis (marijuana) as a 'Schedule 1' drug, supposedly having no legitimate medical purposes (a position that is contrary to almost all bona fide research on the topic and is now in opposition to State law in the majority of the United States). The hypocrisy and logical inconsistencies simply defy reason.

LSD and other psychedelic drugs, outlawed by the Federal government in 1966, remain against the law, although the number of citizens (particularly the young) using these drugs, which are non-addictive and have unique properties of expanding consciousness, is in the millions. The social phenomenon of this use is entirely illicit, and yet the psychedelic experience has positively enhanced the perceptions of many in technological and artistic fields – many, including Steve Jobs, have spoken publicly of this fact.

Hopefully our society will one day mature to the point that the vision of safe, positive psychedelic exploration can be legally available to those whom it might benefit.

Given the nature of the personal experiences of the authors when they were undergraduates at Princeton University, the authors reject the use of hypnosis or drugs for any form of mind control, military or institutional or otherwise. MK-ULTRA, in the opinion of the authors, was a tragic and warped deviation in the field of mind research, conducted in secrecy and intended to have been permanently concealed. The authors paid a price for having been unwitting guinea pigs of a CIA-funded project at a formative time in their development.

The authors believe that our world's psychedelic culture needs to come together as an open community devoted to safe mind exploration. Those having psychedelic experiences and conducting research need to 'come out of the closet,' for they have been yet another repressed segment of society that has been persecuted for over half a century.

The publication of this book is intended as a contribution in that direction.

Please visit this website for further information:

www.blowingamericasmind.com

THE NEW YORK TIMES, THURSDAY, OCTOBER 6, 1988

C.I.A. Near Settlement of Lawsuit By Subjects of Mind-Control Tests

By PHILIP SHENON

Special to The New York Times

WASHINGTON, Oct. 5 — The Central Intelligence Agency appears to be close to settling a lawsuit filed by nine Canadians who sought compensation after discovering they had been unwitting subjects in mind-control experiments, some involving LSD.

Lawyers with knowledge of the case said today that the C.I.A. had agreed to pay nearly $750,000 to the Canadians, who were patients in the 1950's of Dr. D. Ewen Cameron, a psychiatrist at McGill University in Montreal.

Documents that became public in the late 1970's showed that the C.I.A. had used private medical research foundations as a conduit for a 25-year, multimillion-dollar research program to learn how to control the human mind.

A Series of Experiments

Through one of the foundations, the agency funneled tens of thousands of dollars to Dr. Cameron to pay for an array of experiments that involved LSD, electroshock therapy and a procedure known as "psychic driving," in which patients listened to a recorded message repeatedly for up to 16 hours.

Lawyers announced a tentative settlement of the 1980 lawsuit during a hearing today in Federal District Court in Washington.

Officials of the Justice Department, which is representing the C.I.A. in the litigation, said the settlement is subject to approval by senior aides to Attorney General Dick Thornburgh, a process that could take several days or weeks.

James C. Turner, a lawyer for the plaintiffs, said in an interview that the settlement "proved no part of our Government is above the law."

"I think the whole thesis of our case was that this program of human subject experimentation was shot through with negligent and callous diregard of the welfare of the subjects," he added. "It's an ends-justifying-the-means mentality that I hope we've seen the last of."

Bill Devine, a spokesman for the C.I.A., said today that "any settlement, if approved, would not represent a concession of liability on the part of the agency; the agency has consistently maintained that its actions were appropriate at the time."

Asked why, in that case, the agency had agreed to the tentative settlement, Mr. Devine said, "We just believe it's in everybody's interest to resolve it at this time."

The C.I.A. used a front organization called the Society for the Investigation of Human Ecology to help pay for the work of Dr. Cameron, a psychiatrist who directed the Allan Memorial Institute in Montreal. Dr. Cameron died in 1967.

The money was provided to Dr. Cameron as part of the C.I.A.'s effort in the 1950's and 60's to develop drugs or techniques that could control human behavior. The campaign was encouraged by the conviction of some officials that the Soviets and Chinese had developed brainwashing and mind-control devices.

Patients of Dr. Cameron were subjected to a regimen that included heavy doses of LSD and barbiturates, the application of powerful electric shocks two or three times a day, and prolonged periods of drug-induced sleep. According to Government records, the patients and their relatives were not told they were taking part in experiments.

DR. HUMPHRY OSMOND
Guest Speaker
NSID NATIONAL CONFERENCE

B18 SUNDAY, FEBRUARY 22, 2004 · LOS ANGELES TIMES

Obituaries

Humphry Osmond, 86; Coined Term 'Psychedelic'

By Elaine Woo
Times Staff Writer

The boisterousness that came to be called the Psychedelic '60s would have been unimaginable without the likes of Timothy Leary, Peter Max, the Grateful Dead and . . . Dr. Humphry Osmond.

Osmond, who died of cardiac arrhythmia Feb. 6 at age 86 at his daughter's home in Appleton, Wis., was the true father of the turned-on decade. The British-born psychiatrist coined the word "psychedelic" in the early 1950s, after novelist Aldous Huxley asked him for a dose of the hallucinogenic drug mescaline. Despite some fears that history would record him as "the man who drove Aldous Huxley mad," the good doctor obliged, unwittingly setting in motion what would become a massive cultural movement.

Huxley did not go mad, but he did experience a high of historic importance. He detailed his mescaline experience in the 1954 book "The Doors of Perception," which became a bible for such leading 1960s seekers as Leary and philosopher Alan Watts. Their advocacy of mind-expanding, chemically altered states made drug-tripping mandatory for many intellectuals and the generation of youths who identified themselves as hippies — a development that Osmond would deplore as dangerous and irresponsible. Yet the train had left the station, transporting, among others, a young songwriter named Jim Morrison, who, in tribute to Huxley's famous book, named his band the Doors. Osmond's concept of psychedelic went, in a few short years, from his brain to an entire society.

That the moniker for the movement could one day be traced back to an English emigre with sparkling blue eyes and a fondness for Shakespeare was inconceivable in the 1950s, when Osmond was a psychiatrist at Weyburn Hospital in Saskatchewan, Canada. A native of Surrey, England, who earned his medical degree at the University of London in 1942, Osmond was interested in the biochemical roots of mental illness, a focus that had left him outside the psychiatric mainstream in Europe, where Freudian analysis was dominant. He immigrated to Canada, where he found a more hospitable environment for his theories, and later to the United States, where he worked at the University of Alabama and a psychiatric institute in New Jersey.

In 1952 he garnered attention in the medical community with his idea that schizophrenia was caused by the human body's production of a hallucinogenic compound. With his colleague, Dr. John Smythies, he theorized that the compound had properties similar to mescaline and related to adrenaline. "This was a remarkable hypothesis," said Dr. Abram Hoffer, who was director of psychiatric research in Saskatchewan and hired Osmond. Hoffer later became known for his treatment of schizophrenia with megadoses of vitamin B-3 and ascorbic acid, a regimen he said is largely owed to the early work of Osmond and Smythies.

Osmond advocated using mescaline to simulate the experience of schizophrenia in doctors involved in the treatment of those with the disease. Believing that the design of mental institutions was inferior to that of zoos, Osmond gave another hallucinogen, LSD, to architects in the hope that the drug would sensitize them to the spatial needs of psychotics and result in more humane environments.

His interest in the impact of architecture on human behavior stimulated the rise of socio-architecture as a field, said Robert Sommer, a professor emeritus of psychology at UC Davis, who described his former colleague as charismatic and "a Roman candle of ideas: He shot them off right, left and sideways."

Osmond also used LSD to treat hundreds of alcoholics. Among those he administered it to was Bill Wilson, co-founder of Alcoholics Anonymous.

Taking the idea that alcoholics have to "hit bottom" before finding the motivation to stop drinking, Hoffer said he and Osmond thought that LSD, by simulating violent delirium, would help alcoholics "hit bottom in a safe way" and remember enough of the experience to avoid it under any circumstances. After several tries, however, Osmond found he was having trouble giving patients an awful time. "They were enjoying it," Hoffer recalled. "Humphry was seeing a new phenomenon."

HUMPHRY OSMOND

Jim Morrison of the Doors, right, named his band for the book by Aldous Huxley, above right, in which he wrote about using mescaline that he got from Dr. Osmond, above.

Instead of using LSD as a stick, the researchers began to view it as a carrot — one that could produce therapeutic, transcendental insights. They treated 2,000 alcoholics with the drug, 40% of whom stopped drinking and joined Alcoholics Anonymous, Hoffer said.

When LSD was banned in the 1960s, the therapy became moot. But what many experienced as the pleasurable effects of a hallucinogenic drug was an important discovery, one that led Osmond to secure his place in cultural history.

In the early 1950s he was contacted by Huxley, the esteemed British novelist known for his 1932 novel "Brave New World," in which totalitarian rulers chemically coerced the world into submission. Despite that cynical view, Huxley believed in the potential of certain drugs to produce beneficial changes in consciousness. He wished to discover whether he might change his own mode of consciousness "to be able to know, from the inside, what the visionary, the medium, even the mystic were talking about."

Having heard of Osmond's work with mescaline, he made a request: Could the doctor, who was then still in Canada, bring him some of the drug the next time he passed through Los Angeles?

The opportunity came in May 1953, when Osmond arrived in town for a psychiatry convention. Years later, he remembered standing at a table in Huxley's Hollywood home, dissolving the silvery, white mescaline crystals into a glass of water and worrying whether the dose — four-tenths of a gram — would be enough or too much.

Although it did not work as quickly as he expected, the dose proved to be just enough to launch Huxley on what he later described in his book as a splendid inner journey. He perceived the jackets of books lining his shelves as divinely aglow. He felt his being flow into a typing table and a wicker chair. He beheld the flowers in a vase with new eyes, seeing "what Adam had seen on the morning of his creation — the miracle, moment by moment, of naked existence." Mundane objects were so transfigured in his heightened state that Huxley "had an inkling of what it must feel like to be mad."

After the effects of the mescaline wore off, he wrote "The Doors of Perception," a title borrowed from a line by poet William Blake. "If the doors of perception were cleansed," Blake wrote, "everything would appear to man as it is, infinite."

Huxley and Osmond became close intellectual mates. "It was really delightful to see these two men speak so fast about every possible subject," Huxley's widow, Laura, told The Times last week. "They were bouncing all over the universe."

Among the many things they discussed was the need for a new name for substances like mescaline, which then were called psychotomimetics for their ability to mimic the qualities of psychosis in users. Osmond sought a name that de-emphasized the pathological effects and highlighted the wondrous. He had tried the substances himself and pronounced his experiences with them among "the most strange, most awesome and . . . most beautiful things in a varied and fortunate life."

In an exchange of letters, Huxley proposed that the drugs be called phanerothymes, which was taken from Greek and Latin words related to spirit or soul. He incorporated the word in a couplet he sent to Osmond: *"To make this trivial world sublime/ Take half a Gramme of phanerothyme."*

Osmond "thought that was a stupid word," recalled Alex Randall, a former student of Osmond's who teaches communication at the University of the Virgin Islands. "He said, 'That word will never catch on.' "

The word Osmond preferred also had Greek roots, but it meant "mind-manifesting." He replied to Huxley with a couplet of his own: *"To fathom hell or soar angelic/Just take a pinch of psychedelic."*

For Osmond, it was just a short trip from there to posterity.

The 9 historic people portrayed in this book include:

Robert Francis Goheen, President of Princeton (1919 – 2008)

Dr. Humphry Osmond, "Psychedelic Pioneer" (1917 – 2004)

Bernard S. Aaronson, Ph.D., psychologist (1924 – 1990)

Carl C. Pfeiffer, pharmacologist (1908 – 1988)

Timothy Leary, Ph.D., psychologist/philosopher (1920 – 1996)

Stan Sieja, Princeton fencing coach (1912 – 1982)

Dr. Willard Dalrymple, Princeton Infirmary (1921 – 2015)

John Selby (Born 1945 as John Selby Smith)

Paul Jeffrey Davids (Born 1947)

Several characters in this book, inspired by real people who played a role in this story, are composites of various people the authors knew when the main events of the story took place. That list includes Anne, Mike, Anita, Pok, and the authors' other classmates at Princeton.

ARTICLES AND PHOTOS

Questions for Open Discussion

The impact of a good book resonates more deeply and provides new insights if we reflect upon questions about the plot, characters, and themes. The following questions (either on your own or in a group) will help stimulate deep reflection and discussion:

One: The two authors of ***Blowing America's Mind*** did their best to dramatize actual experiences and scenes in Princeton's history. Did you feel they succeeded in honestly bringing to life the actual feel of participating in campus situations during the late sixties?

Two: The CIA was documented doing some very bad things fifty years ago, even to its own citizens. Do you think the CIA has changed its devious ways, or is it still secretly caught up in performing illegal atrocities?

Three: After reading ***Blowing America's Mind***, what are your feelings about hypnosis – is it a positive research tool for unlocking the mysteries of the human mind, or is it a dangerous tool that violates free will and human integrity?

Four: Psychedelic drug use by the younger generations has been growing steadily, even with severe warnings by medical authorities. What are your feelings about LSD, peyote (mescaline), ayahuasca, 'magic mushrooms' (psilocybin) and so on – are they helpful for waking up healthy young minds, or are they dangerous and to be avoided at all cost?

Five: How did you feel in this book about the probable cooperation of Princeton administrators and NIH with the CIA in allowing and administering CIA research using American students – was it essential for America's safety, or a serious breakdown in ethics, freedom, and wisdom?

Six: Jonathan, a main character in ***Blowing America's Mind***, was a social outsider who sought insight and relevance and meaning in consciousness research. Did you respect his life choices and support his sometimes wild explorations, or was he wrong in pushing societal limits and letting his own brain be an internal testing ground for radical methodologies?

Seven: Anne enters the story early, but plays a minor role in the ensuing Blowing America's Mind drama. Linda likewise. Did you feel the female element in the story should have been more important, or was the account well-balanced in portraying the all-male Princeton environment?

Eight: Jeffrey often had to play foil to Jonathan's more mature and wild adventures. At the end of the book, how did you feel about Jeffrey's character – was he overly innocent and passive, or did he hold his own in a challenging new situation?

Nine: President Goheen was an actual historic figure on campus during the 1960's when this story took place. Did the authors disrespect his position and personality, or did you feel they correctly presented him as a struggling conservative administrator caught way over his head in a unique new student situation?

Ten: Currently, judging from the news, there is growing interest in psychedelics worldwide in psychiatric circles, because it seems to help people with PTSD, ADHD, anxiety, addiction, and depression recover from their condition. Do you support psychedelic research in this regard, or are you against it?

Eleven: Marijuana has become a dominant presence influencing our younger generations, as grass strains become much more powerful in stimulating psychedelic experience. In this regard, should our government honor each citizen's right to do what they want with their own inner experience, or continue to maintain laws that make otherwise law-abiding citizens criminals for exploring inner realms of consciousness?

Twelve: Controlling other people's minds and actions through subtle hypnotic techniques and mind-altering drugs is always a temptation for those in power. How do you think we should protect our population against secret power-hungry plots to influence public opinion and behavior?

for blogs, further information and discussions visit
www.blowingamericasmind.com

About the Authors

JOHN SELBY

After Princeton, John worked as a musician, a screenwriter, a teacher, and a therapist. He has also worked in advertising, product development, and mindfulness training. After extended years of travel and writing in South Africa, Mexico, Guatemala and Germany, he married Birgitta Steiner and they moved to Kauai to raise their family. Today, they live in Santa Cruz, California.

Including *Seven Masters One Path*, *Quiet Your Mind*, and *Let Love Find You*, John has published three dozen books on a wide variety of topics, and he has produced many meditation videos plus the MoodLift App. For more information, please visit www.johnselby.com and www.wizewell.com

PAUL JEFFREY DAVIDS

Following his work as production coordinator on 79 of the original animated episodes of "The Transformers" TV shows, and after co-writing six of the "Star Wars" sequel books for Lucasfilm, Paul Jeffrey Davids served as story co-writer and executive producer on "Roswell: The UFO Cover-up" for Showtime. He went on to produce, write and direct "Timothy Leary's Dead," "Starry Night," "The Sci-Fi Boys," "Jesus in India," "The Life After Death Project," "Before We Say Goodbye," "Marilyn Monroe Declassified" and other films for television, most of which were released internationally by NBCUniversal.

Paul is also a noted artist who has had many exhibitions (www.pauldavids-artist.com) and a performing magician. Paul and his wife of 45 years, Hollace Davids (longtime Senior Vice President of Special Events for Universal Pictures), have two grown children who also work in the entertainment business.

For revealing discussions by the authors regarding the various themes of this book; plus enlightening information about these topics; emerging news about present-day psychedelic research and related controversies; and much more concerning mind-manipulation, deep hypnosis, cover-ups and the chemistry and politics of consciousness expansion, join us at our ever-expanding website:

www.blowingamericasmind.com

~~~~~~~~~~~~~~~~~~~~~~~~~~~~~

Printed in the United States of America
~~~~~~~~~~~~~~~~~~~~~~~~~~~~~